Caradoc's Kin

The Craddock Family

of

Cranford, Kettering & Sheffield

J.P. Craddock

First Produced 1995
Second Edition 2006

Third Edition published by Cade Books
©2020 John Peter Craddock
All rights reserved.
ISBN 978-0-9931987-7-9

www.cadebooks.co.uk

Front cover -   Joseph Craddock (1847-1924) Midland Railway driver
with a Johnson 4-4-0 locomotive outside St. Pancras station
detail from an oil painting by Peter Craddock

Contents

Acknowledgements

The author would like to thank the following for their interest and assistance in producing this book –

Helene Allsop, Ian Coddington, Samuel Copnell, Peter Craddock, Philip Craddock, Malcolm French, Christine Hassell, Anne Hodgson, John Milner & Philip Wadner.

- and the staff of the following institutions –
Associated Society of Locomotive Engineers and Firemen; The British Library; The Guildhall Library, London; Kettering Cemetery; Kettering Library; The National Archives; The National Railway Museum; Northamptonshire Record Office; Sheffield Archives; Local Studies, Sheffield Central Library; Society of Genealogists; Stevenage Central Library.

Introduction

Family history researchers often encounter a common problem. There is usually a weakness in relying on each generation to pass on family information. The chain, it is true, is only as strong as its weakest link. However, so long as there is some semblance of a chain, accumulated findings can be used to re-forge the links and thus strengthen the chain. Of course, the new chain will never entirely match the original.

My Craddock family line can be traced back to the eighteenth century in Cranford, near Kettering, in Northamptonshire. For my ancestors Joseph Craddock and his daughter, Sabina, poverty meant having to leave their home village for Kettering and then, with Sabina's two children, to seek relief in the Union workhouse. For Sabina, liberation from that institution led only to the appropriately named Gas Street and, in her old age, a return to the same dreaded workhouse.

However, Sabina's son, also Joseph, joined the Midland Railway Company which took him to Sheffield where he brought up his family and was eventually able to buy two newly-built houses in a more prosperous district. He was, however, not keen that his Sheffield family should learn much about his humble origins in Kettering. (The irony was that he was probably never aware of his wife's much darker family history.) For Joseph, prosperity lay through industry and hard work and that was the path he wished his only surviving son, Ernest, to follow.

It is often said that generals apply the lessons learned in the last conflict in fighting the next war, whilst ignoring the advances made in the interim. This can also apply to parents and the guidance they give to their children. Joseph's intervention in Ernest's early career must have caused some sort of a rift. The passage of time, which included Ernest's Great War service, starting his own family and taking over his father-in-law's coal merchant business, would have helped to bring them back together.

The business provided for Ernest's own family and for his parents-in-law but he knew that was not the way to greater prosperity and he did not want either of his sons to take that route. Parental intervention during the Second World War removed his younger son, Peter, from his grammar school and placed him in a humble, but potentially opportune position in industry. Peter's parents did not take that decision lightly and for Ernest, in particular, it must have brought back memories of his own start to his working life. However, the human spirit usually wins through and makes the best of the situation. Peter did just that and forged a career that took himself and his family to another level of prosperity.

A quarter of a century after 'Caradoc's Kin' was first produced, I have updated the story to incorporate new findings and air fresh interpretations of events. History is never set in concrete. It is forever subject to reappraisal and re-evaluation but must always be set in the context of its time.

John Craddock
January 2020
9 Plash Drive, Stevenage SG1 1LW
johncraddock17@yahoo.co.uk

CHAPTER ONE

Origins

Craddock, the personal name, is as old as British history. As a consequence of this great antiquity there have been many variations of spelling. It means 'amiable' from the Celtic root 'car-', 'to love'.

The earliest recorded bearer of the name was Caradoc, who the Romans called Caractacus. He was the son of Cunobelin who had combined the tribal territories of the Catuvellauni and Trinovantes. (These territories approximate to the modern Hertfordshire and Essex with south Suffolk respectively.) From his capital at Camulodunum (Colchester), Cunobelin governed the expanding Catuvellaunian empire for more than thirty years and established extensive trading links with the Roman continent. Indeed, Cunobelin achieved such wealth and position of power that the Romans came to regard him as the King of the Britons.

When Cunobelin died shortly after AD 40, Caradoc and his brother, who were not as well disposed towards Rome as was their father, proceeded to expand the Catuvellaunian empire still further. They captured the last remaining stronghold of the Atrebates (Sussex) and expelled their king who fled to Rome.

Since Julius Caesar's short-lived incursions of 55 BC and 54 BC, Rome felt that they had unfinished business in Britain. During Cunobelin's reign, trade had flourished between Britain and the Roman continent. In order to maintain this, Rome was prepared to overlook Cunobelin's expansionist ambitions but became wary when this was continued by his vigorous sons. Caradoc and his brother, by creating a threat to the maintenance of a valuable commercial trade, precipitated the enduring Roman invasion of Britain in AD 43.

Caradoc, as chief of the Catuvellauni, based at Calleva (Silchester), was strategically well placed to oppose the Roman legions but he and his brother were nevertheless defeated at the two day battle on the Medway at Rochester and at the crossing of the Thames. With Emperor Claudius' triumphal march into Camulodunum and the Roman consolidation of their claim on Britain, Caradoc and his followers retired to the territory of the Silures (South Wales) from where frequent sallies were made against the encroaching Romans.

Having put down the Iceni revolt and established a Roman colony at Camulodunum, Marcus Ostorius Scapula, the Roman Governor, advanced on the Britons to the west. Caradoc led his British host northward into the territory of the Ordovices (Shropshire) and there on the hill of Caer Caradoc (the fort of Caradoc) a battle took place in the summer of AD 50. (The hamlet of Cradoc in Powys is situated two miles north-west of Brecon.) Despite an energetic defence, the Britons were dislodged from the hill and Caradoc's wife, daughter and brothers fell into the hands of the Romans. Caradoc, however, escaped and took refuge in the territory of the Brigantes (Yorkshire) whose queen, Cartismandua, betrayed him to the Romans. Caradoc and his family were taken to Rome and paraded before Claudius who was so impressed with the British leader's undaunted bearing that he granted him and his family their lives. With the legendary flourish of 'Why do the Romans, who possess such palaces, envy the poor huts of the Britons?' Caradoc disappeared from history.

The name Caradoc was revived by General Sir John Francis Cradock, 1st Baron Howden, of Peninsular War fame who changed his surname to Caradoc by Royal licence in 1831. His only child, Lieutenant-General Sir John Hobart Caradoc, 2nd Baron Howden, married but had no children so that on his death in 1873 the barony of Howden became extinct.

The village of Craddock in Devon is situated one and a half miles east of Uffculme. It derives its name from the brook, Carducc, which in turn was derived from the personal name. In 1185 the village was called Cradocumba and in 1249, Cradok. The personal name of Craddock is of such antiquity that the usual rule that locality surnames are derived from place names is turned on its head.

With the proliferation of the use of surnames from the thirteenth century and the increased keeping of written records, instances of the name multiplied. Early references to Craddock as a surname are found in pipe rolls of 1177 in Herefordshire, 1185 in Glamorgan, 1187 in Shropshire and 1205 in Worcestershire. Subsidy roll references include 1296 in Sussex and 1301 in Yorkshire.

Northamptonshire references to the surname date from at least as early as the 1538 will of Richard Cradocke of Cottesbrooke, ten miles to the north of Northampton. Analysis of the earliest references to the surname Craddock and its variations of spelling in Northamptonshire conclude that bearers of the surname are generally to be found in the centre of the county.

At Hardwick, equidistant from both Cottesbrooke and Northampton, lived Peter Craddock, a miller, and his wife, Cassander. The couple's two sons were Richard, christened in 1593 in Hardwick, and Thomas christened three years later in Burton Latimer five miles to the north-east. Following Peter's burial in 1615 in Hardwick no further trace of the family has been found but they may well have been the ancestors of the Craddock family of Burton Latimer.

Later records tell of another Thomas Craddock of Burton Latimer. He married twice, first to Elizabeth Keach in 1716 and second, after Elizabeth's death, to Anne Middleton in 1720. Despite begetting at least six children, this Craddock family line was not maintained in Burton Latimer much beyond Thomas' death in 1739 aged forty-seven. His eldest son, Thomas, moved to Lowick, eight miles to the north and his line continued in the parish into the nineteenth century. Another son, William, is believed to have founded the extensive Craddock family of Great Harrowden, four miles to the south.

William's younger brother was christened John on 24th April 1726. Since nothing further is known of this John neither in Burton Latimer nor elsewhere, and other candidates in neighbouring parishes have been ruled out, it is believed (but cannot be proven), that this was John Craddock of the adjacent village of Cranford near Kettering – the earliest known member of the author's family line.

CHAPTER TWO

Cranford under the Old Poor Law

The village of Cranford lies four miles to the east of Kettering in the county of Northamptonshire.

Originally called Craneford because cranes (or herons or storks) once frequented the ford, prior to 1954 the village comprised two parishes, Cranford St. Andrew to the north and Cranford St. John to the south separated by a stream called the Alledge which feeds the Nene at Thrapston. In the Middle Ages, the Alledge, which was then wider, marked the boundary between the Dioceses of Lincoln and Peterborough. St. Andrew's church was in the Lincoln Diocese, St. John the Baptist's church in the Peterborough Diocese. Both churches date from the reign of Henry II.

At St. Andrew's church on 8th October 1758 John Craddock of the parish of Cranford St. John and Sarah Creek of the parish of Cranford St. Andrew were married by the minister, the Rev. John Hargreaves, in the presence of Thomas Holman and John Hargreaves Junior.

John Craddock was 'of the parish of Cranford St. John' at the time of his marriage because he had gained settlement in the parish. This was most likely to have been attained by a year's unbroken employment in Cranford St. John. (John was not baptised in either of the Cranford parishes and, furthermore, there are no Craddock entries in the Cranford registers prior to 1758.)

John was an agricultural labourer for all of his working life. He and his family probably owed their livelihood and home in Cranford St. John to the Robinson family who had owned most of Cranford since the previous century. The Robinsons lived in Cranford Hall, an early Georgian mansion that overlooks parklands close to St. Andrew's church. Most of St. Andrew's inhabitants were workers at the Hall Farm but it was common for families to move freely between the two parishes.

The labourer's life was a hand-to-mouth existence of long days in the fields and interminable winters. When they became sick or too old to work they looked to the parish for support. The poor rate was levied on the landowners and well to do of the parish and administered to the needy by the Overseer of the Poor.

Means of employment were limited in the rural community. The Constables Account Book for Cranford St. John records that some villagers received payment for killing vermin – polecats, foxes, hedgehogs and sparrows - towards the end of the eighteenth century. Indeed, between 1775 and 1777 William Craddock received payment for sparrows at the rate of 2d per dozen. William was John and Sarah's eldest son and it appears that he was in some sort of trouble as a warrant for 1s was served on him in July 1780.

On 1st November 1787, William, or Bill, was given 7/6 to visit a doctor in Dallington near Northampton – a thirty mile round trip. Thirteen days later he was given a further 10/6 to visit a doctor in Harringworth – the same distance in the opposite direction. His condition was not recorded but there can be little doubt that it was from that affliction that he died the following month. Bill was in his twenty-fifth year and unmarried. Mr. Deston, the Coroner received 6/8 from the parish.

Poor relief was not only paid to the needy. Those who had rendered some sort of service could also benefit from the fund. Consequently, on 26th July 1790, Sarah Craddock received 4/6 for nursing 'Oliver's child' who was ill until the end of August 1790.

During his final year, John Craddock drew upon the poor fund on three occasions, including 1st October 1791 when he received £2 14s to pay his rent. When he was buried in St. John's churchyard on 16th January 1792 Mary Surton and Oliver's wife were paid 3s to assist with his funeral arrangements. In addition, two women, probably Mary Surton and Oliver's wife again, received 5s for laying John out and for other expenses. John's coffin and two hundred (240 planks) of wood cost 11/4.

After the death of her husband, Sarah became heavily dependent upon poor relief and she received sums of between 6d and 1/4 each week. When she was ill between April and July 1793 these rose to between 1s and 2/6 per week. Occasionally relief was provided in kind and on 14th February 1795 Sarah received a basket of coals.

John and Sarah Craddock's second son, John, married Hannah Meadowes in 1798 in the neighbouring parish of Barton Seagrave. The marriage register describes the younger John as being 'of this parish' indicating that he had then gained settlement in Barton Seagrave. The couple had no children and it was John and Sarah's third son, Michael, who maintained the family line.

When Michael Craddock was betrothed to Ann Franklin, a Cranford spinster, banns were published in Ann's parish church, Cranford St. Andrew, on 20th November and 5th and 12th December 1790 and in Michael's parish church at Great Harrowden on 19th and 26th December 1790 and 2nd January 1791. It is interesting that Michael's parish was then Great Harrowden. There can be no confusion of identity since Michael was the only contemporary Craddock bearing that Christian name to be found in the county. Since Michael was then in his twentieth year his example (and that of his father before him) demonstrates the labourers' mobility from their parish of birth. Michael would have acquired settlement in Great Harrowden by virtue of being employed in the parish for an unbroken year. Since it is likely that Michael's family was then closely related to the Craddock family of Great Harrowden his settlement lends weight to that connection.

As the eighteenth century drew to a close Michael's mother became increasingly dependent upon parish poor relief. In September 1797 Sarah was very ill and the following year she received 2/6 per week, the next year, 3/6 and in 1800, 4/6. On 10th April 1802 she received 2/6 to have her shoes mended and from 7th February 1803 she was provided with a pint of beer each day. The beer was carried to Sarah by Mary Witney and Sarah Holland who were initially paid a half-pint of beer each for their service. Later they were paid 9d rising to 1s each. During that winter, on both 13th and 19th February 1803, Sarah also received beer from her 'waiters' and monetary relief in March when the Overseer's account book was filled. The next book is missing from the series so that details of Sarah's death and burial on 15th April 1803 have been lost.

Cranford was enclosed in 1805 – the year of the battle of Trafalgar. Both events would have figured little in the life of the Craddock family, but for families who owned animals, enclosure of the commons was very significant indeed.

Cranford St. Andrew's Poor Book states that Michael Craddock's wife, Ann, was provided with 1s on 4th April 1812. This payment was related to her confinement with their youngest child since the next month a statement was made to that effect when she received an additional 5/6. From at least as early as that year the family became regularly dependent on poor relief and on 19th May 2/6 was given 'to Michael Craddock by order of Sir George Robinson for loss of time in obtaining and attending a summons for relief'.

On 28th June Michael and Ann's daughter was christened with her mother's name in St. Andrew's church. (The younger Ann was known as Frances or Fanny in later life.) The previous day it was recorded in the Poor Book that 5s was paid 'to Craddock by order of Magistrate'. A week later, on 4th July, 'nothing to Craddock' was written. Presumably these statements relate to Michael's appeal for relief.

From at least 6th May 1815 Michael Craddock was paid between 1s and 7s a week by the parish whilst he was 'on the round'. With the depression of agricultural prices following the Napoleonic wars, labourers' earnings fell below subsistence level. The Roundsman system involved sending unemployed labourers around the parish in search of work whilst their wages were subsidised by a parochial allowance. This left the labourer partly employed and partly supported by the parish. In 1817 Michael was on the round at Linnell's farm.

From 3rd May 1817 Michael also received money whilst 'on the road' – presumably for mending roads. On 16th August he received 2s extra on account of his wife's illness and Michael was working partly on the round and partly on the road when Ann died. She was only forty-five and their youngest child was five years old. Mrs. Freeman and Mrs. Newbury laid Ann out and she was buried on 31st August in St. Andrew's churchyard. Her coffin was provided by John Abbott at a cost of 17/6 to the parish. A 'bell and grave' cost another 3/6.

The year after his mother's death John Craddock, Michael and Ann's third son, joined his father on the round and the road. He was then about eighteen. John's younger brother, Charles, was only thirteen when he received his first shilling 'on the round' in 1824. Their elder brothers, Joseph and William, do not appear in the payment records so it is presumed that they then had fully paid employment.

Michael Craddock received up to 10s a week when he was ill or lame. In February 1824 he broke a finger and Dr. M. Chard was paid 10/6 for setting it. Two years later Michael visited the infirmary (presumably in Kettering) to receive treatment for his lameness. 'Caution money' of £1 was deposited by the parish as surety for his good conduct.

On 9th June 1827 Michael was provided with 4/2 for sixteen days on the round. Five days later Ben Holbert received 2/3 for 'being at Craddocks 3 weeks cooking his victuals'.

At the beginning of 1828 Michael's son, Charles, was lame. Two weeks later Michael was ill and he and 'his boy' (who was then seventeen) received 3/6. Michael's illness was to last a good month and recurred the following winter when he was laid up for eighteen days. For the latter Michael received 8s. Charles remained on the round until at least November 1828.

On 18th July 1818 a Sarah Craddock was paid 2/4 for attending to Ann Grey's girl. Sarah's identity is unknown but she was evidently a relative because when she married John Carter on 13th October 1819 in St. John's church the witnesses were Joseph Craddock and John Sharp. Joseph Craddock was Michael and Ann's eldest child and Sarah Craddock may have been a member of the Great Harrowden branch of the family. Then, on 1st November 1819, Michael Craddock married the above mentioned Ann Grey, a Cranford widow, in the presence of his son Joseph Craddock and John Sharp.

The second Mrs. Ann Craddock provided lodgings for a few weeks each spring. From mid-March to the beginning of April 1825 Ann received 1/6 a week for putting up Mary Abbott. In 1827 from mid-March to mid-April Mary was joined by Sarah Betts (or Bates) for which Ann received 2/3 a week. The following year Sarah was the only lodger and Ann's payment was again 1/6.

Seventeen days after his father's re-marriage, on 18th November 1819, Joseph Craddock also married a widow, Eleanor Johnson, at St. John's church in the presence of Eleanor's brother, Edmund Toy, and John Sharp.

Eleanor Johnson was the eldest daughter of William and Sarah Tye (Tighe or Toy) and about nine years Joseph's senior. In 1801 Eleanor married William Johnson and in the period to 1814 the couple had eight children who were all christened in St. Andrew's church. However, despite this apparent continuity of attachment to the village, sometime during this period William gained settlement in the parish of Finedon, four miles to the south of Cranford. When William became ill in 1813 money was advanced by the Overseer of the Poor in Finedon to the Cranford Overseer to cover the expense of taking him to the infirmary. The following year William died and money was similarly advanced to pay for his burial in St. John's churchyard. From 1816 money was also provided by the Finedon Overseer to 'Widow Johnson' and to two of her older children, Abraham and William, who were then living in Finedon and aged eleven and nine years respectively. During at least the next fifteen years the Johnson brothers lived in Finedon whilst they received poor relief for the cost of lodgings, being provided with work, assistance when they were sick, clothing, and the washing and mending of the latter. Such was the brothers' attachment to Finedon that both married there.

Whilst Eleanor was relieved of bringing up two of her children during her widowhood she must have appreciated the assistance of her second husband. However, despite her re-marriage 'Widow Johnson [of] Cranford' continued to receive poor relief from the Finedon overseers until 1830.

By Joseph Craddock Eleanor bore two more children, baby Joseph who was christened in 1821 (and of whom nothing more is known) and, following the family move to Cranford St. Andrew, their daughter Sabina who was christened in St. Andrew's church on 30th March 1823. Sabina has always been an uncommon Christian name. Perhaps Joseph and Eleanor's daughter was born on 29th August of the previous year – St. Sabina's Day.

Life cannot have been easy for Joseph with both his own family and some of his wife's family to support. Employment was intermittent and the Churchwarden's Account book for Cranford St. Andrew records that in March 1828 Joseph received payment for working on the churchyard road.

Being her youngest half-sibling's junior by nine years and only eight or nine when her mother died in 1831, Sabina Craddock must have had a disjointed childhood. As the Johnson children made their own ways in the world Joseph and Sabina became the only occupants of their home in Cranford St. Andrew.

1886 1 FOOT : 1 MILE

TRAMWAY

Cranford St. Andrew

St Andrew's Church

St John's Church

Cranford Hall

Manor House

Red Lion (P.H.)

Cranford Station

Rectory

Foot Bridge

Signal Post

CHAPTER THREE

Cranford under the New Poor Law

In accordance with the Act of Settlement of 1662, settlement in a parish was generally gained by place of birth or by a year's unbroken employment in a parish. Having acquired the right to settle, the parish was then committed by the Poor Law Acts of 1597 and 1601 to certain responsibilities, including the relief of their poor. As a consequence the paupers' mobility was restricted since other parishes were reluctant to accept any additional burden. Settlement certificates were issued to legitimise parochial responsibility and removal orders could be invoked for the forcible eviction of undesirables.

The Poor Law Amendment Act of 1834 radically altered the situation. The New Poor Law Act abolished outdoor relief to the able-bodied and their families and the old system of workhouses was revised to become the primary method of relieving the poor. In order to be effective, conditions in the workhouse and the associated stigma had to be severe enough to deter all but those truly in need. It was not sufficient merely to be poor in order to qualify for relief; the able-bodied had to be demonstrably destitute.

In accordance with the new Act, Boards of Guardians were established as the bodies of townsmen responsible for dealing with the poor. Each Board was responsible to the Poor Law Board commissioners in London and to the magistrates. Parishes were grouped into Unions and each Union was required to provide a workhouse of sufficient capacity to cater for the whole Union. The parishes of Cranford St. John and Cranford St. Andrew were placed in Kettering Union.

In 1839 Joseph Craddock's house in Cranford St. Andrew was included in the parish valuation. His house, that did not have a garden, had a rateable value of £1 precisely. Typically, houses with gardens then had a rateable value of £1 15s. Cranford Hall had a rateable value of £83 6/8. The then incumbent of the Hall, the Rev. Sir George Stamp Robinson, 7th baronet, owned most of the parish properties including Joseph and Sabina's home.

On Sunday, 6th June 1841, the day the census was taken; Joseph and Sabina were visited by Mary Halbard, a girl of Sabina's age. Mary was the daughter of William and Sarah Halbard of St. John's parish and as consequence of her visit she was listed twice in the returns.

At the beginning of the nineteenth century the population of Cranford was 419. By 1841 it had risen to nearly 600 but from then on the population declined as the labouring classes were compelled to abandon the countryside for the employment provided by the expanding towns. Joseph and Sabina were of this number and Kettering was their destination.

Joseph and Sabina would have been familiar with Kettering because Sabina's uncle, Edmund Tye and his family lived in the town. (Edmund was Eleanor's brother and a witness of her marriage to Joseph in 1819.) In January of the following year Edmund married Mary Chapman in Newton-in-the-Willows, three miles to the north of Kettering. The couple's first children were born in Newton, the youngest in Kettering. From at least 1841 the family resided in Gas Street from where Edmund worked as a silk weaver.

Kettering of the 1840s was dirty and unsanitary. It was ill-lit and unhealthy and was without water and sewerage systems. With the expansion of the town the poor were forced into any accommodation they could find. The close proximity of strangers would have subjected Joseph and particularly Sabina to pressures beyond their experience.

On 18th May 1847 Sabina gave birth in Kettering to a baby boy who was named Joseph after his grandfather. Unfortunately for young Joseph he was born into the world both illegitimate and poor.

During 1846 and 1847 the elder Joseph's brother, Charles, and other men received payment for the occasional work of carting and breaking stone for the roads of Cranford St. Andrew. Apparently, Charles ceased this work in July 1847 but in December of that year Joseph joined John and Thomas Scott digging stone for the roads. Early in the New Year the three were joined by Joseph Saddington and Joseph continued to work on the roads until February.

During the week ending 26th August 1848 Sabina received 5/8 in money and the equivalent in kind from Kettering Union for herself and her child. This outdoor relief was provided in Cranford St. John where Sabina's grandfather Michael also received outdoor relief for being not able-bodied. There were then, for a brief period, four generations of this Craddock family line in Cranford. During the first two weeks of September Sabina received about 1/6 in money and the equivalent in kind.

On 22nd June 1850 Sabina gave birth at Swan Street in Kettering to a second illegitimate child who was named Susannah. (She was later known as Susan.) Swan Street was then a cottage area that contained the Swan Inn. Later the cottages were replaced by shops and the road renamed Montagu Street.

There is no record of Sabina's children's father or fathers and no evidence that the family received any support from that quarter. Sabina was unmarried with two young children. The elder Joseph was approaching sixty and infirm and in November Kettering Union received £1 caution money for him. The family was in a dire situation.

With his eldest son and his family in Kettering, Michael Craddock continued to live at London End in Cranford St. John with his wife and daughter, Frances Newman, and her family.

Michael was widowed for the second time in 1842 and six years later, from the week ending 25th March 1848, he received between 2/6 and 5s in money and the equivalent in kind from Kettering Union. Michael was categorised as 'not able-bodied' and 'irremovable poor', meaning that he was exempt from having to enter the workhouse in Kettering and that he could receive outdoor relief in Cranford.

When Michael died on 28th December 1848 his neighbour, Mary Rowley, informed the registrar. Mary was also 'not able-bodied' and in receipt of both money and kind from Kettering Union. Michael was buried in St. Andrew's churchyard on New Year's Eve 1848. His funeral expenses of 22s were paid for by Kettering Union.

Michael Craddock was survived in Cranford by Joseph's brothers, William, John and Charles. William appears not to have married. John married Frances Whitelock in 1824 and Charles married Ann Threadgold in 1835. By 1838 Charles and Ann were renting a house in Cranford St. John that was owned by Mrs. Battle. There they brought up their three sons, Benjamin, William and John. Benjamin and William had large families. William married Zilpah Claypole in 1861 and their eldest son Arthur, who lived to the age of ninety, was the father of Norman Craddock. Norman, who died in 1995 and his wife Betty, who died in 2004, were the last members of the Craddock family to reside in Cranford.

St. Andrew's Church

St. Andrew's School

Northall Bridge

Tannery

Mission Ho.

Gas Works

Westfield

Albert Works

Hill Side

Manor House

Royal Iron Works
(Agricultural Implements)

St. Peter & St. Paul's Church

Cattle Market

CEMETERY

Stamford House

Longdale

South Lodge

Southlands

Belle Vue

Carey Cottages

Kettering Union Workhouse

Station

Goods Shed

Ground

K E T T E R I

KETTERING 1884   1 FOOT : 1 MILE

17

CHAPTER FOUR

Kettering Union Workhouse

Kettering's parish workhouse was situated in Workhouse Lane in the very heart of the town. It was administered by the Vestry who tried expedient after expedient to maintain some form of cottage industry such as weaving and lace making in the workhouse.

Kettering Union however was seventy-seven square miles in extent encompassing thirty parishes, including the two Cranford parishes. Since the parish workhouse was inadequate to cater for the poor of the Union it was decided to build a new institution on London Road, about half a mile from the town centre. Kettering Union workhouse (now St. Mary's Hospital) was built of sandstone between 1836 and 1838 to Sir George Gilbert Scott's design at a cost of £6,000.

In 1849 the Union workhouse could accommodate 250 inmates. Administered by a Board of Guardians which met weekly, each pauper cost the Union 3s 2½d per week. Everyone feared the Union. If you went there you were considered to be beyond hope.

The workhouse would have been the first public building the Craddock family saw as they entered the town from Cranford and by the spring of 1851 the elder Joseph, Sabina and her children, Joseph and Susannah, were residing within the workhouse walls. The gulf between the Britain of the Craddock family and the Britain of the Great Exhibition in Hyde Park in that year could not have been wider.

Whilst it was of no consolation to the family, they, and in particular Sabina, were perhaps comparatively fortunate. In 1833 Kettering Quarter Sessions court committed a woman who had produced successive illegitimate children to the House of Correction in Northampton for three months. Magistrates would occasionally order mothers of illegitimate children to be examined. When such examinations revealed the identity of the father, a bastardy bond could be issued compelling him to contribute to the child's maintenance. In December 1840 Kettering Board of Guardians gained orders and payments from the fathers of three illegitimate children then in their care. The New Poor Law however, with the emphasis upon indoor relief to be received in the workhouse, meant that it was no longer required that the fathers of illegitimate children should be traced.

Kettering's Board of Guardians was always reluctant to impose the full rigour of the new Poor Law Act to the running of the Union workhouse. According to the letter of the Act, husband and wife were to be housed in separate quarters for the purpose of ensuring that the pauper population was not increased. Movement to and from the institution was not prohibited, only restricted. Visiting times were also limited. Kettering Union workhouse gained a humane reputation in these respects. However, the inmates left the institution in the same state that they entered it – penniless.

During the Craddock family's stay in Kettering Union workhouse the master was Henry Kilby and the matron, his wife Lucy. According to the census of Sunday, 30th March 1851, there were then 117 inmates residing in the workhouse. They were listed, where possible, in families. The Cranford contingent was listed together, headed by Joseph Saddington, a widower with three children. Sabina appeared next along with her two 'natural children', Joseph and Susannah, aged three years and nine months respectively. They were followed by three orphans, Charlotte, David and George Patrick aged eight, six and four years. The elder Joseph Craddock completed the Cranford group indicating that Sabina had taken the Patrick children under her wing. The latter were the children of John and Susan Patrick of Cranford St. Andrew. John Patrick died of dropsy in the spring of 1850, his wife of a debility in the following November.

This was a turbulent time for Kettering Union workhouse. Shortly before the census was taken, the porter, Joseph Hawthorn, was dismissed for 'using improper language to the inmates'. This was later qualified in the Poor Law Board correspondence as 'for general bad conduct'. A few days later the schoolmaster and schoolmistress, Charles Warren and Elizabeth Brown, were suspended from their duties after the master discovered they were having an affair that resulted in the schoolmistress's pregnancy. On 1st April the Poor Law Board accepted their resignations and they left. A week later John Howes, latterly a sergeant in the Royal Horse Artillery, was appointed porter. Later in the month, Wheeler Stephen and his wife Louisa Mary were appointed schoolmaster and schoolmistress.

In October the workhouse school was inspected by H.M. Inspector of Parochial Union Schools. Papers examined related to religious knowledge, spelling, penmanship, arithmetic, grammar, history and geography. In addition, the inspector assessed the pupils' reading, industrial skill, the skill of the teachers and the general state of the school. Skills such as lace making and knitting were taught to the female inmates.

On Christmas Day the inmates were treated to roast beef and plum pudding. In addition, the females were given tea and cake by Miss Roberts. This must have been a pleasant relief from their usual fare and labourers such as old Joseph were provided with a quart of beer each day.

The Poor Law Board correspondence for October 1856 provides dietary tables for pauper children aged between two and nine years residing in the workhouse. Since young Joseph and Susan were then in this age group the details are of particular interest. For breakfast the children had bread and milk porridge. Dinner comprised a carefully weighed portion of one or two of the following – bread, beef, potatoes, soup and suet pudding. Supper was bread and cheese.

The means by which the Craddock family escaped the workhouse may be gleaned from the story of one of Kettering's leading citizens.

John Turner Stockburn was born in 1825, the only son of Joseph Stockburn, a Kettering draper. In later years John claimed that he went to no fewer than ten schools – the first being the Dame's School in Cranford. From 1840 John was apprenticed to the drapery trade in Canterbury and on his return to Kettering in 1844 he entered his father's business in which a Mr. Goosey was a partner. Their premises were situated in the High Street and when Joseph Stockburn retired in 1846 his son continued in business with Goosey.

Following John's marriage to Eliza Osborn Smith in 1852, the couple lived above the drapery shop. Over the next twenty-six years the couple had seventeen children though only seven survived infancy. In 1856, with his brother-in-law Robert Wallis, John introduced the first sewing machine to Kettering and commenced stay and corset manufacturing.

1857 witnessed two significant events in the history of Kettering: the opening of the Leicester to Hitchin railway line (and the town's railway station) and the collapse of the Gotch Bank. The Gotches were a very prominent Kettering family who had attained their position by establishing what was for a time the only boot and shoemaking business in the town. It also became the largest in the county before the collapse that enforced the sale of the firm to meet the claims of the bank's creditors. Although this was devastating to their many employees, the occurrence ultimately brought fresh opportunities to Kettering as new firms sprang up. The fortunes of the district improved markedly and the footwear trade began to flourish, not only in Kettering but also in the neighbouring towns and villages.

J.T. Stockburn was one of many to prosper in the wake of the Gotch Bank collapse and that same year he purchased his father's drapery shop and the following year the Carey Mission House in Lower Street, one of the most imposing residences in the town. This house, which was where the Baptist Missionary Society was founded in 1792, was his home for the next sixty-four years and a base for his family, social, business, political and religious life. In his early thirties, Stockburn had established himself as one of Kettering's leading citizens.

As he prospered as a manufacturer, Stockburn's non-conformist upbringing drove his involvement in social reform. He had a long-term interest in the poor of the town and of the welfare of the inmates of the workhouse.

It is quite possible that Sabina Craddock and her children owed their escape from the workhouse to the activities of J.T. Stockburn. In accordance with the doctrine of the times, this would not have been a purely humanitarian act. Following his lead, others, including other members of Stockburn's family took up his ideas so by 1862 the underwear and clothing industries were well established in Kettering. Those businesses required labour and cheap labour was to be found in the workhouse. The elder Joseph was too infirm to be of value to an employer and since the money Sabina could earn as a lace maker would not support her father as well as herself and her children he had to remain in the workhouse.

From at least 1851, Sabina's cousin, Mary Tye, the daughter of Edmund and Mary Tye of Gas Street, had been a stay stitcher. The family connection with the trade may also have been influential in gaining employment for Sabina.

Life in the workhouse must have been a dismal existence. The inmates had few opportunities to taste life outside and were permitted, at most, a single visit each week from relatives and friends. Some left periodically to taste freedom before returning to the institution. Not to do so could invite melancholia or worse. It is presumed that Sabina's third illegitimate child was conceived in the town. Ellen, as her daughter was named, was born on 10th June 1857 in the workhouse perhaps because Sabina required the institution's maternity facilities.

Since the 'Father's Name' entry of all three of Sabina's children is omitted from their birth certificates and baptismal entries the identity of her children's father or fathers may never be discovered with absolute certainty. However, it should be noted that young Joseph was ten years old when his younger sister was born. If he did not know his own father he could possibly have known Ellen's.

However, with the growth of DNA databases, in the foreseeable future it may be possible to link this family to another family that then resided in Kettering. The ancestry of third, or more distant, cousins of the author could then indicate the identity of Joseph's father. Similar work conducted by descendents of Susan and Ellen may then be able to establish whether they were full or half siblings of each other and their brother.

Whilst his family enjoyed their freedom of a sort, the elder Joseph remained in the workhouse and that is where he was when the 1861 census was taken. A survey of inmates taken that year states that Joseph had spent precisely nine years in the workhouse due to his infirmity. That is, during the past decade, Joseph had spent only a year outside of the workhouse walls.

Joseph was later joined in the workhouse by his brother William who died there in October 1862. Joseph died in the workhouse on 12th October 1862 aged seventy-one. The following day William's body was buried in Cranford.

The family connection with the workhouse was next taken up by Joseph and William's brothers, John who died there in 1868 and Charles, who died there in 1883. Thus, in the absence of alternative care for the elderly, all four of the sons of Michael and Ann Craddock of Cranford died in Kettering Union workhouse.

CHAPTER FIVE

Gas Street to Darley Dale

By the spring of 1861 Sabina Craddock and her children, Joseph, Susan and Ellen, were lodging in Gas Street, Kettering. The head of their household was Elizabeth Ashton, the elderly widow of a Chelsea pensioner. Mrs. Ashton's seventeen-year old grandson, David Ashton, also resided in the house on the day the census was taken. Later, Mrs. Ashton entered the workhouse where she died in January 1862.

Gas Street, which in earlier times had been called Mill Lane and Goose Pasture Lane (and is now called Meadow Lane), is a steep road running down from the High Street. Kettering Gas & Coke Company, which had lit the town since 1834, was situated on a quarter acre plot at the lower end of the street next to the railway. Despite the benefit to Kettering in general, the works provided a smoky countenance that gave Gas Street its name.

There were at least two reasons why Gas Street became the family home following their escape from the workhouse. Firstly, it was a poor quarter of the town comprising dwellings surrounding a court containing a communal water pump. Secondly, Sabina's uncle, Edmund Tye and his family then lived in Gas Street. Edmund was widowed in 1848 and by 1861, he and his son David were lodgers in the household of his daughter and son-in-law, John Woodcock, a blacksmith.

During the early years in Gas Street Sabina would have worked at home whilst she cared for young Ellen. The pittance she earned from lace making would have been supplemented by the contributions of her older children. Joseph, who was then in his teenage years, worked as a labourer for one of the nineteen farmers in the town and Susan, who was three years his junior, was employed as a domestic servant.

Sabina's livelihood was clearly uncertain because when Ellen was christened at the age of seven at the Church of Saints Peter and Paul in 1864 'No Profession' was stated for her mother in the baptismal register. Susan was nearly sixteen when she was christened in 1866. Sabina was again without employment. (No record of Joseph's christening has been found.)

From 1857 when the Midland Railway Company opened the Leicester to Hitchin line and the first trains rattled through the new station, a fresh vitality coursed through Kettering.

In February 1858 trains of the Derby based Midland Railway were connected, via the Great Northern Railway, to Kings Cross in London. The railway brought prosperity to industry, mobility for the masses and an influx of workers from the length and breadth of the country. One of the latter was Edward Milner.

Edward Milner was the second son of John and Mary Milner of Darley, near Matlock, in Derbyshire. John Milner worked a fifty-acre farm of pasture, arable and meadow at Tinkersley, on the hillside to the north of Darley. Since it was likely that the tenancy of the farm would ultimately pass to his elder brother, Edward Milner left Darley to make his living elsewhere.

In October 1868 Edward joined the Midland Railway Company as a horse driver at Kettering station with a wage of sixteen shillings. He was nominated by a Mr. Needham who performed a similar service for other recruits. Being brought up on a farm, Edward would have been acquainted with horses so he would have been well suited to his job of hauling goods between the station and the town.

At that time there was no road that led directly from the station to the gas works. Coal for the works had to be unloaded from railway trucks onto horse drawn wagons, hauled up Station Road, along Sheep Street, through the Market Place, into the High Street and down Gas Street. Tree-lined Station Road was built by the Midland Railway with a uniform gradient and surfaced with cobbles so that the horses could get a grip. Gas Street was unmetalled so hooves and wagon wheels churned it into a quagmire in wet weather. (The situation did not improve later when traction engines replaced the horses.) By regular activity around the town Edward Milner became acquainted with Gas Street and its residents.

To Joseph Craddock, labouring each day as generations of his family had done before him, a job on the railway must have presented an attractive proposition. Edward Milner would have earned almost twice Joseph's wage and had far greater prospects. Encouraged by the example of Edward and other railwaymen, in February 1871 Joseph travelled to Sheffield where he commenced work as an engine cleaner with the Midland Railway Company.

By the spring of that year Edward Milner was lodging in Gas Street with Robert Torrell, a railway fireman, his wife and young daughter. William Tebb, who was also a fireman, was also staying with the family on 2nd April, the day the census was taken. Edward was then a pointsman based at the new signal box at Kettering station (which was replaced in November 1870) or at Kettering Junction.

From the beginning of the railways, legislation dictated that a signalman, a position that had evolved from that of pointsman, switchman and other related grades, be nominated by three directors of the company and then be appointed by at least two Justices of the Peace. Edward must have gained a reputation as a responsible employee to have attained such a position. His wage of twenty-one shillings would also have eased his financial situation and to Susan Craddock he would have been quite a catch.

The 1871 census describes Sabina, Susan and Ellen Craddock as stay makers living in Gas Street. At this time much of Kettering was a community of out-workers. Basic training would have been provided in Stockburn's premises in Richards Leys or Tanners Lane, both of which were close to the Stockburn residence in Lower Street. Then the processes of wadding, joining etc. would have been carried out at home.

Edward Milner and Susan Craddock were married at the Parish Church of Saints Peter and Paul on 25th June 1871 in the presence of William Collis and Ruth Newman. (Ruth was Sabina's cousin from Cranford.) Susan was described as a machinist in the marriage register implying that she was then working in a factory.

After the nuptials the couple lived with Sabina and Ellen in Gas Street and whilst they were there their first child, Annie, was born. Tragically, Annie was afflicted with a wasting condition and she died aged only two weeks. On 15th September, Susan had the heart-rending task of registering both the birth and the death of her first child.

By the end of the year Susan was expecting again and the couple moved to their own home, a terrace house in West Street, a short distance from Gas Street.

West Street has existed from Kettering's earliest days as a cobbled enclave of about twenty houses to the west of the Market Place. Twelve of the houses on the south side of the street were rebuilt in about 1870. George Herbert Milner, who was born in July 1872, and Harry Milner, who was born in December 1873, entered the world in one of those houses.

Before his younger son had attained his first birthday, Edward's job had moved to Miller's Dale, about five miles to the east of Buxton, in Derbyshire. Edward remained a pointsman but with a wage of twenty-three shillings. The young family – Edward, Susan, George and Harry – left West Street and journeyed north, by way of the Midland Railway, to Blackwell Mill and their new home amongst the Derbyshire hills.

According to his granddaughter, Margaret Billingham, Edward Milner used to walk through a railway tunnel as a short cut. In the course of his duties Edward must have walked the two miles of track between the signal boxes at Miller's Dale Station and Miller's Dale Junction. This stretch of line contains Chee Tor tunnel (495 yards) and Rusher Cutting tunnel (121 yards).

Fred Milner, born in September 1876, was the only child of Edward and Susan to be born whilst the family lived at Blackwell Mill. By the time of Fred's christening, in Kettering on 10th June 1877, the family had moved down the line to Rowsley.

March of 1877 witnessed many new railway developments at Rowsley. Up and down sidings were opened as well as the South Junction signal box. Edward appears to have taken the opportunity of working at Rowsley to house his family within a mile of his father's farm at Tinkersley. Unfortunately, the move cost Edward a shilling of his wage – a reduction from 24s to 23s. The Midland Railway Company staff records describe his position as that of signalman, but since that grade had evolved from that of pointsman, his duties would not have significantly changed. According to Margaret Billingham, Edward worked at Rowsley South Junction signal box, adjacent to 'Nanny-goat' crossing, until he retired in about 1910.

In March 1878 Kate, Edward and Susan's oldest daughter to survive infancy was born. She, like her brothers, was taken to Kettering to be christened. At the beginning of 1879 Edward's wage was again reduced by a shilling. The reason for this is unknown but the railway companies made widespread use of fines for the most trivial of offences. However, two months later his shilling was restored. With the arrival of Edith in January 1880 the Milners would have had to account for every penny.

The census taken in April 1881 finds the Milner family residing in Deeley's Cottages in North Darley (which were demolished in about 1950). The three eldest children – George, Harry and Fred, aged 8, 7 and 4 respectively – were described as 'Scholars', and their sisters, Kate and Edith, were aged 3 and 1. The boys would probably have attended the infants' school in Two Dales, a mile or so to the south-east. Registers and log books for the school have not been found which is unfortunate since the increasing number of Milner siblings may have produced some comment even in an age of large families. The next additions to the family were Willie, born in October 1881, and John, known as Jack, born in July 1883.

The Milner children were brought up in the Wesleyan Methodist faith and the next three, Lizzie, Bertha and Mary Jane (known as Jennie), were born between 1885 and 1888. By the latter date the family had moved to Two Dales. It is likely that they moved directly to 4 King's Row (later called King's Terrace) on Park Lane. (This address was also referred to as Rye Croft.) Tragically, Bertha lived only a year.

The census, which was taken on Sunday 5th April 1891, presents an interesting picture of the Milner family in Two Dales. Edward and Susan were listed with their children – George Herbert, 18, a railway labourer; Harry, 17, a domestic servant on the Stancliffe Estate; Fred, 14, a nursery labourer; Kate, 13; Edith, 11; Willie, 9; John, 7; Lizzie, 6; Mary Jane (Jennie), 2 and Edward (Ted), 1. Arthur born on 22nd August 1891 and Walter, nearly three years later, completed the family. Thankfully, by this time the older children were beginning to make their own way in the world.

The winter of 1894/5 was exceptionally severe and Darley was covered with deep snow. All outside workers on the Stancliffe Estate were laid off and Harry Milner, no doubt influenced by his father and older brother, joined the Midland Railway Company.

Harry travelled up the line to Manchester where later in March 1896 he joined the Grenadier Guards. Two years later Harry participated in the Sudanese campaign that culminated in the Battle of Omdurman in 1898. The following year he was recalled from the reserve and served in the Boer War. On leaving military service Harry married Isabella Wright and they brought up their four children in Bolton.

The oldest surviving Milner sibling, George, became a driver on the Midland Railway. His son Edgar, known as Eddie, was born in Normanton in Yorkshire, married and lived in Dundalk in the Irish Free State for a few years prior to the

Second World War. He then moved to Manchester where he worked for the Singer Sewing Machine Company until he retired. Eddie's son John and his wife Jill live in Melton Mowbray.

The last surviving Milner siblings to live in Darley Dale were Edith, Ted and Jennie. Edith died in 1955. Ted worked as a clerk for a firm of Matlock solicitors from the age of fourteen to that of eighty and died in 1974 in his eighty-fifth year. Jennie married in 1914 but tragically became a widow of the Great War. She died in 1977 the day before her eighty-ninth birthday.

Left – Susan & Edward Milner, circa 1920

Right – Private Harry Milner of the Grenadier Guards, circa 1896
detail from an oil painting by Peter Craddock

CHAPTER SIX

Kettering to Australia

With the departure from Kettering of Joseph in 1871 and the Milner family three years later, Sabina and Ellen lived alone in their Gas Street home. Although the railway had taken their family far away it also gave them mobility so that Joseph and the Milners were able to return from time to time.

On 10th June 1875 Ellen attained her eighteenth birthday. For a young lady, that occasion marked her official entry into society. The earliest known photograph of a member of the family, which was preserved by the Milner family, records Ellen's debut. It was taken by Alfred Knighton, self-styled 'Artist-Photographer' of High Street, Kettering. Commercial directories indicate that Knighton practised from this address between 1874 and 1876 and, according to the Victoria and Albert Museum, Ellen's dress and hairstyle match the period precisely. The photograph is of particular interest since it indicates that Sabina and Ellen were not as poor as one would otherwise have imagined. If the dress was hired for the occasion, the hairdresser's and the photographer's fees must still have amounted to a fair sum.

In 1876 J.T. Stockburn built the corset factory in Northall Street. The building was constructed in stone in the vigorous Victorian style with blue slate with iron finials and with an 'S' monogram over the doorway. Generally, girls worked at the factory whilst older women did wadding and joining at home. The rear of the factory site butted on to the back garden of the Mission House – the Stockburn family residence.

J.T. Stockburn paid his workers himself each Friday afternoon as he enquired about each of their families. The workers were pitifully poor but

Stockburn endeavoured to assist those in the greatest need – including the financing of nursing care for some families. At Christmas Stockburn compiled a list of the elderly needy and he gave each married couple four shillings and each single person two and six. The money took about three weeks to distribute and his daughter was instructed to tell her father about each individual.

Stockburn's wife used to regularly send items to the workhouse for the benefit of the inmates. A charming story that has passed down through the Stockburn family relates to an exchange between a grocer and Mrs. Stockburn when the latter bought some oranges to take to the workhouse. The vendor, aware of the destination of the fruit, offered some cheap oranges. Mrs. Stockburn's reply was recalled as, 'Young man, if you did not often have an orange would you not like the best when you did?'

On Christmas Eve 1880 Ellen Craddock married John Kennedy at the Parish Church of Saints Peter and Paul in the presence of John's sister and brother-in-law.

John Kennedy was the son of Charles and Jane Kennedy of the parish of Odell in Bedfordshire and was, like his father and older brother, a carpenter and joiner by trade. John was employed all of his working life by the firm of Messrs. Margetts and Neal that later became J.C. Neal Ltd., builders and contractors of Station Road, Kettering.

At the time of his marriage John was lodging at 82 Alexandra Street on the other side of the town. Following the nuptials the couple lived with Sabina at 9 Gas Street and it was there that the couple's two sons, Charles and Arthur John, were born in 1882 and 1883 respectively.

In about 1890 an outing was organised for the workers of Stockburn's corset factory. Vehicles were hired from Billy Briggs of Tanners Lane and about seventy people were conveyed to Lilford Hall off the Thrapston to Oundle road, a journey of about thirteen miles. The group spent a pleasant couple of hours touring the grounds, stables and aviaries. After tea some played games whilst others strolled around the park. When it was time to leave they gathered by the Hall to thank Lord and Lady Lilford for their kindness. On their way home they spent an hour or so at a Thrapston inn. A group photograph was taken to mark the occasion. There is little doubt that the tall figure in the back row captioned 'Mrs. Kennady' [sic] is Ellen. The event took place shortly before she left the firm's employ. The outing, which was recalled by the readers of a Kettering newspaper nearly forty years later, confirms the link between the Craddock family and Stockburn's firm.

The 1891 census returns record the Kennedy family as living at 53 Albert Street, a road running adjacent to Alexandra Street. John Kennedy was listed as the head of his household which comprised his wife, Ellen, their sons Charles and Arthur, and Ellen's mother, Sabina Craddock.

Albert Street and the adjacent roads were developed by Stockburn and the houses were let to his workers. Since there was then a property qualification to vote, some of the residents of the new houses felt inclined to show their appreciation to their employer by voting for the Liberal Party of which Stockburn was a leading supporter. Indeed, in 1892 Stockburn only narrowly lost to Lord Burghley, the Conservative candidate for the North Northamptonshire seat in Parliament.

According to the 1891 census returns 54 Albert Street, which was presumably the house opposite the Kennedy household, was occupied by members of the Tye family. Sabina's uncle, Edmund Tye, died in 1866 and in the late 1880s his daughter Mary, the widow of John Woodcock, and her extended family moved from 29 Gas Street to 54 Albert Street. In 1891, Mary Woodcock, who was Sabina's first cousin, was the head of the household. The residential link between the Craddock and Kennedy families and the Tye and Woodcock families had extended from Cranford to Gas Street to Albert Street over most of the century.

During 1896 Sabina, who was then seventy-three, received six pounds ten shillings old age relief from the Kettering Union. Two years later she received six pounds eleven and six. The spectre of the workhouse loomed ever closer.

The original workhouse infirmary comprised only two rooms, one for men and the other for women. All nursing care was provided by the master and matron in addition to their other duties. Mainly due to Dr. Dryland's efforts a new infirmary and laundry were built in 1894 at a cost of ten thousand pounds. (These were later supplemented by a chronic disease ward and a tuberculosis sanatorium.) Despite these additions to the structure, the workhouse that Sabina, her young children and her father had entered nearly half a century before was the same building that Sabina re-entered in 1899.

A likely reason for Sabina's return to the workhouse was probably the deterioration of Ellen's health due to breast cancer. John Kennedy would have been hard pressed to earn a living whilst nursing his wife and caring for his elderly mother-in-law.

Susan Milner and her family (who then lived in Two Dales near Matlock) maintained their visits to Kettering and would have done what they could. Susan's youngest daughter, Mary Jane, known as Jennie, in later years remembered her horror at being left to nurse her aunt Ellen. As a 'thank you' she was given a chair which she took back home on her own on the railway.

Although a contemporary writer referred to 'the beautiful hospital at Kettering Union' it was nevertheless dreaded because going there was proof of one's poverty. The workhouse, 77 London Road, was however the only refuge for poor people who were sick or aged.

In 1899 Arthur Sattin was the workhouse master. He lived at the top of the tower that was the central feature of the London Road frontage. He gained an autocratic reputation as a result of his attitude towards other members of the workhouse staff. Having retired to his rooms in the evening he would place an oil lamp in his window as a signal for one of the nurses to bring him a cup of coffee or a newspaper.

Another feature of the workhouse that was contemporary with Sabina's residence there was that hedgehogs were kept as pets in the kitchen for the purpose of attempting to keep the cockroach population under control. The dining room walls were hung with still-life pictures of fish, loaves, meat and fruit. A tramp called Patrick painted a picture in return for a night's lodging.

By the close of the century Sabina was totally reliant on the workhouse. During the year ending Lady Day (25th March) 1900 Sabina had received 355 days of maintenance, in 1901, 364 days.

The celebrations marking the coronation of Edward VII would have been a highlight of Sabina's declining years. Due to the King's illness the coronation was postponed from June to Saturday, 9th August 1902. The workhouse was decorated with an archway over the entrance surmounted by a crown under which were the words 'God bless the King'. The outside of the building was illuminated by fairy lamps and Chinese lanterns and decorated with streamers.

The day before the coronation a tea party and entertainment were organised at the Victoria Hall in Gold Street for Kettering residents of sixty-five years and more. In all, 160 women and 122 men attended where they were accommodated at seven long tables.

Although there is no actual evidence that Sabina was present, the facts that she was then in her eightieth year and permanently residing in the workhouse increase the likelihood that she was. (The workhouse inmates were regularly provided with treats such as a ride into the country for a picnic. The coronation tea would have had a strong workhouse contingent because the staff would have encouraged the elderly inmates to attend.)

J.T. Stockburn attended the gathering and was asked to say a few words. Having congratulated so many on being able to take part in the celebrations, Stockburn commented that he had attended the celebrations for Queen Victoria's coronation and, like a great many of those present, he did not expect to see another.

The next day a coronation service was held at the Parish Church followed by a procession through the town and an open-air tea-party for the children. The weather that day was gorgeous and after tea the celebrations, which had adjourned to the forty-acre field close to the Headlands, culminated in a spectacular firework display.

In 1903 there were 282 inmates in the workhouse which was over twice the population of the 1850s. It was there, in the workhouse infirmary, that Sabina died of senile debility on 7th April 1904. She was eighty-one years old.

That day John Kennedy registered her death and stated that his mother-in-law was the 'Daughter of John Craddock, Gardener domestic of Cranford St. John'. Since John had not known Sabina's father the substitution of John for Joseph is understandable. Perhaps Sabina had described her father's occupation thus.

Sabina was buried four days later, on 11th April 1904, in grave number 823 of Kettering Cemetery at a service presided over by the Rev. H.H. Rumsey, a curate at the Kettering Parish Church. The fee of one shilling was donated by the friends of the church. It was never marked by a stone.

Ellen Kennedy outlived her mother by only two months. On 15th June 1904 she died of carcinoma of the breast and exhaustion at the family home, 7 Wyatt Street. She had just turned forty-seven. Three days later she was buried in grave number 640 in Kettering Cemetery – close to that of her mother. The inscription on her gravestone bears testimony to her suffering.

Affliction sore, long time she bore.

Physicians were in vain.

Till God did please to give her ease

and free her from her pain.

Six weeks after his mother's death, Charles Kennedy, then a shoe clicker, married Sylvia Jane Fletcher at St. Mary's Church in Kettering.

Seven years later, in February 1911, John Kennedy married Annie Elizabeth Simpkin at Fletton, which lies about a mile to the south of Peterborough. Annie Elizabeth was twenty years John's junior, the daughter of Edward Simpkin, a railway guard. According to Charles' half-brother, John Edward Kennedy, Sylvia, or Syl, disapproved of her father-in-law's re-marriage. Between 1913 and 1919 the couple had three sons and two daughters – half siblings of Charles and Arthur Kennedy. However, this relationship was little more than academic since by that time, Charles and Sylvia, followed by Arthur, had emigrated to Australia.

In December 1911 Charles, described as a farmhand, and his wife Sylvia boarded the P.&O. ship *Commonwealth* at the port of London. Eight weeks later they arrived at Melbourne in Australia.

After John Kennedy's re-marriage 7 Wyatt Street was maintained as the family home and it was there that he died on 29th November 1931 at the age of seventy-seven. Three days later John's body was borne to Kettering Cemetery by men from the builder's yard where he had worked for nearly sixty years and placed in Ellen's grave. The family home then passed to John's youngest child, Edward, whose home it was until his death in 1981.

Arthur John Kennedy served an apprenticeship as a carpenter and joiner at J.C. Neal Ltd., where his father was the foreman. When the 1911 census was taken

Arthur was lodging with Christopher Orton, a fellow woodworker, and his young family in Sheffield. Judging by the children's places of birth it seems likely that Arthur had accompanied the family to the steel city a year or two before. The following year, in June 1912, Arthur boarded the *Otranto* at London and joined his brother and his wife in Australia.

Having settled in Melbourne, Arthur met Hilda Margaret Polglase in 1916 and they became engaged to be married. That October Arthur enlisted as a Private in the 58th Battalion, 8th Division of the 1st Australian Imperial Force. After being trained as a Lewis gunner, early in 1917 he was sent to England where he received further training at Hurdcott Camp near Salisbury. On the Western Front Arthur saw action at Polygon Wood in Belgium where he received a severe wound to his head, his helmet saving his life. Following treatment at a hospital in France in November he was transferred to Harefield Hospital in England before being sent back to Australia.

In April 1918 Arthur was declared medically unfit for further military service and was discharged from the army and in November he and Hilda Polglase were married at the Wesley Church in Melbourne. Arthur and Hilda set up home at 8 Marlborough Street, Caulfield, where they lived most of their lives, and their only child, Phyllis Margaret Kennedy, was born in 1922.

Hilda Kennedy died in 1968 aged seventy-eight, Arthur Kennedy died in 1971 aged eighty-seven and their daughter Phyllis Watkins died in 1994. Phyllis's children, Helene Allsop and Donald Watkins, have maintained the family line in Australia.

Left – Ellen Craddock, 1875

Below – Employees of Margetts and Neal, builders and contractors, Station Road, Kettering, circa 1895

John Kennedy is standing third from the left

His younger son, Arthur Kennedy, is sitting on the ground at the front

CHAPTER SEVEN

Midland Engineman

Joseph Craddock, Sabina's only son, left Kettering and travelled to Sheffield where he set to work as an engine cleaner with the Midland Railway Company on 7th February 1871. The date is significant since it was just over a year after the Company completed the line from Chesterfield to Grimesthorpe which includes the 1 mile 264 yard long Bradway Tunnel.

As his train made the five mile long, 1 in 100 descent down Heeley Bank and pulled into the Midland station, Joseph must have marvelled at the sights and sounds of the industrial city in much the same way as his mother and grandfather had viewed Kettering a quarter of a century before. Sheffield, the steel city, however, was far removed from Kettering and its cottage industries.

By the spring Joseph was lodging in the back house of 4 Garter Street, off Carlisle Street East, a poor area in industrial Brightside only a few hundred yards from Grimesthorpe engine shed. The householder was Christiana Hodgkinson, a widow with two young daughters. Another engine cleaner, George Noble, who was a couple of years Joseph's junior, also lodged in the house. Mrs. Hodgkinson's husband had been a steel works labourer until his death two years earlier.

The back-to-back was a poor dwelling. At least those in Joseph's household had direct access to the water closet in the back yard. For the Crookes family in the front house a visit entailed a walk along the street, a turn down the side passage and along the back to the shared facility.

As was the practice of the day and was insisted upon by the Midland Railway Company, Joseph's lodgings were within a mile of his place of work, the Grimesthorpe engine shed. Number 25 on the Midland network, the shed was opened in 1861 and replaced in 1877. It had a roundhouse with a 46 foot diameter turntable and outside a 60 foot diameter turntable. After it was opened in 1901 Joseph would have also become acquainted with Ecclesall engine shed (number 25A) at Millhouses which provided the Midland Railway's passenger and mixed traffic locomotives. Engine sheds invoke images of grime and heat and dangerous machinery. Whilst these were certainly present in Joseph's day, the Victorian railway companies and, in particular the Midland, maintained an order of discipline alien to later generations.

Few records of locomotive staff have survived from this era. For the dates of the salient points of Joseph's career the author is indebted to Joseph's granddaughter, Margaret Robinson, whose family retained a remarkable scrap of paper. The scrap is the top portion of a page from a notebook on which Joseph had written the five prominent events, with dates, of his railway career. Joseph had signed the record and the scrap was torn out of the book leaving only a tiny fraction of his signature and what appears to be the incorrect statement that he was twenty-two years old on 15th August 1871. Presumably this is a draft or a copy of his railway service record. According to the scrap, Joseph received his book of company rules in March 1872. By that time he had been cleaning engines for over a year.

Locomotives were cleaned by a gang under the supervision of a senior cleaner. Having been allocated an engine one of the junior members of the gang would be sent to the stores to draw cleaning materials of cotton waste and oil. Upon his return the gang leader would distribute the materials and set each member to work on a particular area of the locomotive being careful to leave himself the easiest task. The procedure was to dip an oily ball of cotton waste into water and draw letter 'S's over the paintwork. This was then rubbed with a clean piece of waste.

Having completed a locomotive the gang's work would then be inspected by a foreman who ran his hand over carefully selected areas such as between the spokes and under the footplate. The standard of work required was most formidable and it was no idle boast that the Midland Railway Company claimed it had the cleanest engines in the world.

Contemporary engine cleaners in Sheffield usually served between four and five years before being promoted to fireman. Joseph must have displayed promise since he was a cleaner for just two years. Being older than the norm would also have acted in his favour and in February 1873 he commenced his firing duties.

The locomotive fireman probably donated more hours of unpaid labour to his company than any other grade. Although no allowance was made in the company procedures for him to do so, the fireman had to attend to his engine long before the appointed time in order to prepare it for the day's work. By the time the driver had arrived to commence his customary circumnavigation of the locomotive with his oil can, the fireman would have checked it over, sought assistance for minor repairs and ensured that boiler pressure could be raised by the allotted time.

According to Ian Coddington, his family recalled that Joseph served as fireman to his great-great-grandfather, Richard Stone. Both being born in 1847, Richard Stone was appointed fireman before Joseph, and since their family lives later converged, it appears that they must have worked well together.

On the Midland the fireman knew his place and kept to it. The footplate of a steam locomotive could support only one boss and it was a bold fireman who questioned the orders or actions of his driver. An express locomotive consumed up to half a hundredweight of coal per mile – half a hundredweight a minute at sixty miles per hour. On some runs the fireman would only bend his back once and then straighten it again as the train coasted into the depot. The toil was unremitting. It required a supple back, hard muscles and stamina to match. On top of that physical effort the fireman was also expected to observe signals on his side of the track.

Before the fire could be fed the coal had to be broken into manageable chunks with a pick and brought forward to within easy reach. Then by 'flashing the blade' of his firing shovel, the coal was distributed around the firebox in a manner calculated to obtain the maximum heat. As coal was emptied from the tender it had to be shovelled forward. Thus much of it had to be lifted twice. The rare achievement of scraping the last scraps from the tender was known as 'clearing the deck'.

The Midland Railway's locomotive superintendent, Matthew Kirtley, died the year, 1873, that Joseph commenced his firing duties. This is significant because the following year the new superintendent, Samuel Waite Johnson, added side-sheets to locomotive cabs thereby helping to protect footplate personnel from the elements.

On 1st January 1875 the Midland Railway Company abolished its 2nd class grade for passengers. All 2nd class carriages were made 3rd class and were provided with upholstered seats to replace the wooden ones that Joseph would have had endured on his journey from Kettering.

Promotion from fireman to driver depended upon seniority, his driver's reports, and regular attendance at work, the condition of the locomotive, smartness, punctuality and perfect eyesight. The last, that had to be maintained throughout his career, was the stumbling block for many a prospective driver. In an age of steam locomotion, oil lamps and flare torches, it was a minor miracle that any man could retain the required standard of eyesight. Drivers of steam locomotives were never allowed to wear spectacles.

The eyesight test was conducted by a variety of means on the Midland Railway. The ability to distinguish the number of dots on blocks of wood with each eye at a distance has been recorded as a contemporary test used at Sheffield.

In addition, the prospective driver was also subjected to a practical examination. This usually comprised taking a part of the locomotive to pieces and making adjustments to the satisfaction of the inspector. Joseph evidently conformed to these requirements and, after six years of firing, on 8th February 1879, he passed as driver. (In Sheffield at that time the norm was six to seven years as a fireman before promotion to driver.)

Railway employment was in many ways a double-edged sword. On the one hand it was a job for life and security of employment was one of its greatest assets. On the other hand the railway companies insisted that all of their employee's time belonged to them. The men had to live within calling distance of the depot, usually within a mile, and he had to be available for work at a moment's notice. (Only when the caller-up was satisfied that the railwayman was awake would he leave the doorstep.) Furthermore, in most other trades the skill of the workman was considered to be equally valuable wherever he was employed. In the case of the driver however, his knowledge was essentially limited to his particular line or network. As track layout and signalling systems became ever more complex, his skill became increasingly specialised. It was this intimate knowledge of their lines, enabling men to recognise landmarks by shape and sound alone, which allowed trains to keep to the time-table despite the severest of fogs or blizzards. It was the recognition of these skills that led to the founding of the driver's craft union.

On 7th February 1880 William Ullyot enrolled in Sheffield as the first of the original thirty-five members of 'The Proposed Society of Enginemen & Firemen'. This later became the Sheffield No.1 Branch of the Associated Society of Locomotive Engineers and Firemen, or ASLEF. The Sheffield branch was thus the earliest ASLEF branch. (During the next five months branches were founded in the following centres, Pontypool, Neath, Liverpool, Leeds, Bradford, Tondu and Carnforth.) The entrance fees were five shillings for enginemen and two shillings for firemen. The first book of minutes and payments to the Sheffield branch states the following for 27th March 1881:

Proposed by Horatio A. Nelson, seconded by John Mason that Joseph Craddock and Joseph Sharpe become members of this society, carried.

That same day John Mason offered himself as general secretary. The minutes record that this was highly approved by the members.

Three months later, on 3rd July 1881, Richard Stone joined the union. He was proposed by Joseph Sharpe and seconded by John Mason. The engine driver Joseph Sharpe and his family lived at 33 Hunsley Street in 1881, three doors away from where Joseph Craddock was lodging at the time.

On 11th September Joseph Craddock received the Society's first rule book. Richard Stone received his on 12th March 1882. In the year when the Midland Railway Company introduced its crimson lake locomotive livery, on 2nd December 1882, Joseph became a registered driver. In order to save money, in 1910, the crimson lake was replaced with a black livery for goods locomotives.

Joseph reaped the benefit of ASLEF membership at least as early as 1883 when he received sick pay. (This information was provided by the General Secretary of ASLEF in London.) Joseph received sickness benefit from ASLEF throughout his term of membership though only records of the later payments have survived. Between 1905 and 1919 these were sums of between 6s 8d to £3 6s 8d per year.

The Midland Railway Company prided itself on the maintenance of the highest of standards in all respects of railway operation. Most Midland employees conformed to the required discipline and conducted themselves accordingly. However, despite that, around 1886 the Midland began a reign of terror against its enginemen. Fines were imposed for minor offences such as delaying a train for a few minutes, mechanical failures and for coal falling off a tender.

Since a week's wage would only be paid when a week's work had been completed, the guaranteed week ensured that the company was obliged to provide a full week's work. By this time Joseph had achieved the top rate after five years service as a driver on full pay: 7s 6d a day. According to regulations issued on 15th July 1887 by the locomotive superintendent from 5th August Joseph could be called on duty to find that his services were not required. In that case he would receive a quarter of his pay. The abolition of the guaranteed week precipitated the first Midland drivers' and firemen's strike for forty years.

On 5th August 1887 without consulting anyone, ASLEF included, the Midland men failed to turn up for work. At that time one third of Midland enginemen belonged to ASLEF. After taking legal advice concerning the company's action in abolishing the guaranteed week, three days later the union made the dispute official by calling out its members. ASLEF was then accused of encouraging the Midland men to strike. Although ASLEF decided not to provide strike pay it insisted that its members would not work whilst non-members were striking over conditions of service.

The company broke the strike by bringing in unorganised enginemen from other areas costing ASLEF dearly in providing out-of- work pay. The strike briefly threw the Midland Railway Company into chaos and cost ASLEF £3,000 but the membership was increased. The year 1887 was henceforth known in railway circles as 'the year of the Midland strike'. Its memory caused resentment for a generation.

In the absence of information to the contrary, Joseph apparently had a railway career free of serious accidents or other misdemeanours. However, any such incident could have provided a glimpse of his working life. The local newspapers provided a wealth of detail and little was considered too trivial to be recorded.

Related information could also have been recorded in ASLEF's Locomotive Engineers & Firemen's Monthly Journal the first issue of which appeared in February 1888.

Infringements of Midland Railway Company rules were recorded in pedigree books. From 1901 these contain the railwayman's name, crime and penalty. An earlier volume is solely an index of names and pedigree numbers with the occasional mention of a depot. One book records a J. Craddock, which may refer to Joseph, and an E. Milner of Rowsley Station, who was certainly Joseph's brother-in-law.

Comments made by George Fletcher, a Sheffield driver of the generation after Joseph, were recalled by Joseph's grandson, Stanley Craddock. According to George, Joseph, known as 'Joe' to his workmates, had a reputation for being able to really push a locomotive along. The Midland paid their top link express drivers 3d a day extra for a ten hour day.

Joseph's niece, Olive French, remembered that her uncle and her father, Tom Merrick, drove all types of trains. Tom, who retired in about 1935, received a wage of £3 15s including his London expenses. When in London, they lodged over-night in 'barracks' for which Tom received an extra 5s allowance. Lodging was widespread on the Midland and their premises were to be found in all the major railway centres. In 1914 the 158 mile run from Sheffield to London took three hours. Tom and Joseph used to drive to London and to Scotland about twice a month.

Despite the availability of privilege tickets for both the employee and his wife, it did not apply to their children, and some, Tom Merrick included, claimed that they could afford neither the time nor the cost of taking their family on holiday. Joseph, however, could, and he took his Sheffield family the length of the Midland network to Bournemouth on at least one occasion.

Joseph Craddock's 'CV'
Preserved by the Robinson family

Group of Sheffield Midland Company enginemen and their families, circa 1905
Tom Merrick (with the bowler hat) & Joseph Craddock (with cap)
are the tall central figures standing next to each other
Tom's wife, Tilly Merrick, is the third lady from the right
Tilly's son, Charlie Cripps, is lying on the ground

CHAPTER EIGHT

Hunsley Street

Joseph lived as a lodger during his first decade in Sheffield. According to his niece, Olive French, he lived with a family by the name of Gascoyne in Sheffield and occasionally with his sister, Susan Milner, and her family in Derbyshire.

Joseph and Susan and members of their respective families maintained close contact throughout their lives. However Joseph's contact with his family in Kettering was distant in more than proximity. His duties with the Midland Railway Company would have taken him back to Kettering on a regular basis when he would have had the opportunity to visit his family. It appears that Joseph maintained contact in that manner with the result that his own Sheffield family knew little of his Kettering family and, presumably, vice versa.

According to Joseph's daughter-in-law, May Craddock, he was occasionally teased at his apparent lack of family background. The fact that he was born out of wedlock, his mother's unusual Christian name and her town of residence was passed on to succeeding generations. However, nothing else, beyond the relationship to the Milner family was forthcoming. Ellen Kennedy and her family were nearly forgotten. Joseph's son, Ernest, joked to his eldest daughter that his grandmother worked in a stately home and that, in view of his father's illegitimacy, they might be related to aristocracy. This was clearly a 'leg-pull' but is indicative of Ernest's lack of knowledge concerning his father's background.

When the 1881 census was taken, Joseph was lodging at 27 Hunsley Street in Grimesthorpe, the home of George Clarke, his wife Hannah and Hannah's daughters, Catherine, Mary Ann and Matilda Howell, known as Kate, Polly and Tilly, twenty-four, twenty and eighteen years old respectively.

The Howell family came from Kinver in Staffordshire. Hannah Hobson married Thomas Howell, an iron puddler, in Amblecote in 1856 and their first two daughters were born in Potter's Cross and christened in Kinver. According to Thomas and Hannah's granddaughter, Olive French, Thomas had difficulty finding employment and as a result of the family's wanderings the couple's youngest daughter was born in Glasgow.

By 1864 the young Howell family had arrived in Sheffield. Thomas was employed as a puddler at John Brown's Atlas steel works in Brightside where the mass production of railway rails was pioneered. Aged thirty, Thomas became acquainted with a fellow worker, a twenty-year-old Irish lad by the name of Anthony Duggan. On Saturday, 6th August, the pair had spent the evening drinking and gambling in Wilson's dram shop in the Old Haymarket and both arrived back home to Carlisle Street in an intoxicated state early on Sunday morning. Under the impression that Thomas owed him half a crown from a bet, Duggan followed him home to no. 2 court from where Hannah pushed Duggan out of their house and locked the door. Duggan, however, refused to leave and made a noise outside and knocked on the windows. Thomas took the door key from the mantel piece and went out to confront Duggan, closely followed by Hannah who did her best to keep the pair apart. A fight ensued during which Duggan hit Thomas under his right ear. Duggan said 'How do you like that, Tommy?' Thomas was picked up and carried into his house but despite the rapid appearance of a Dr. Barker, he was declared dead. When apprehended, Duggan said that he was very sorry that Thomas had died and that if they had not both been drunk it would not have happened. The coroner's jury returned a verdict of manslaughter against Duggan and in the West Riding Assizes Crown Court the judge sentenced Duggan to two months imprisonment.

That terrible night left Hannah and her daughters both devastated and destitute. Kate was nearly eight, Polly, four and Tilly, less than two years old. Away from potential support from their family in Staffordshire, Hannah then had to take on the burden of keeping their house and home. It must have come with some relief, when Hannah married George Clarke at Christ Church in 1869. George was also an iron worker and a few years younger than Hannah. When the 1871 census was taken the family, all listed with the surname Clarke, lived in Forncett Street, a road running parallel to Carlisle Street East. Times were still hard since they shared their home with two male lodgers who were only a year or two younger than George. Kate and Polly having been christened in Staffordshire, Tilly was baptised at All Saints, Brightside, in June at the age of eight.

A decade later, the family's lodger, Joseph Craddock, found life with the Clarke couple and the Howell young ladies very agreeable. This is evident since on St. Valentine's Day 1882 Joseph married Kate Howell at Christ Church, Pitsmoor. It is stated on the marriage certificate that Joseph's father was 'John Craddock', 'Labourer'. That relieved Joseph of the stigma of illegitimacy on that public record. It is likely that he never became aware of his wife's much darker family secret which must have haunted Kate for the rest of her life.

After their marriage Joseph and Kate lived at 22 Botham Street (a road that ran parallel to Hunsley Street) and it was there that their first child, Edith, was born on 12th October 1883. Nearly two years later on 21st August 1885 Ethel was born at 31 Hunsley Street. On 26th November 1887, the couple's first son, Joseph Henry, was born at 65 Hunsley Street. Tragically, the baby boy contracted smallpox aged only six days and he died a week later. There were over four hundred deaths due to smallpox in the 1887/8 outbreak in Sheffield.

Just over a year later there was another tragedy in the family when Ethel contracted measles and she died in January 1889 aged nearly three and a half. Whilst infant mortality was high and parents had to be prepared for such a loss, it was particularly tragic that Joseph and Kate lost two of their three children. However, later that year another daughter, Nellie, was born to Joseph and Kate on 1st August 1889. The memory of Ethel was retained by the siblings she never knew. Nellie and her brother were taught to refer to floating dandelion seeds as 'angels' and the children wondered whether one of those could have been 'Our Ethel'.

A year or two after Nellie's birth a young man with a West Country accent started engine cleaning at the Grimesthorpe engine shed. Tom Merrick was his name and he was to become a prominent figure in Joseph's professional and family life.

Oliver Thomas Merrick was born in Congresbury, twelve miles west of Bristol, in 1870. Oliver was the son of Thomas and Sarah Merrick who lived at Canal Terrace in Bathampton, three miles north-east of Bath.

According to Olive French, her father started work at the age of eleven as a cellar boy in a large house in Bathampton eventually rising to the rank of valet. A photograph has been preserved of Oliver sitting next to the driver of an open landau. He was wearing doe skin breaches, high boots and a tall hat with a cockade up the side. Olive French recalled a curious story that the owner of the house decided that he would only employ male servants of at least six feet in height. Since her father was half an inch short of that mark he was obliged to seek employment elsewhere.

Despite this shortcoming (pun intended), Oliver must have been highly regarded by his former employer and their circle as he was presented with four books with dated inscriptions from distinguished persons from October 1885 to September 1889.

Bath was at the south-western extent of the Midland Railway network. Late in 1890 or early in 1891 Oliver Merrick journeyed north to Sheffield where he commenced work as an engine cleaner at Grimesthorpe engine shed. From then he was known by his contracted second Christian name since 'Tom' would clearly be more acceptable to his new railway fraternity.

In Tom Merrick, Joseph found a young man in just the position he had been in twenty years earlier. Joseph took him to 97 Carlisle Street where he introduced him to Charles Cripps and his daughter-in-law, Tilly, the youngest of the Howell sisters. Tilly had married Charles' son Harry in 1883 and they had two children, Charlie and Hetty. Harry Cripps, who was a labourer in an iron works, died of heart disease at the age of thirty in August 1890 leaving Tilly with two children to support. Tilly was a dressmaker and she also took in washing and sewing to make ends meet. By introducing Tom to the Cripps household Joseph found Tom homely lodgings and provided the Cripps family with additional income.

At this time Tilly's mother and step-father, Hannah and George Clarke, were living at 12 Draper Street. They shared their three roomed home with their eldest grandchild, George Copnell, and two lodgers. Both lodgers were of a similar age to Tom Merrick, both were then engine cleaners and both had been born in Batheaston, which is about a mile to the north of where Tom was born. Clearly, the three young men had travelled from Somerset together and they had all found lodgings in the households of Joseph's wife's family.

By 1893 the Cripps family and Tom Merrick had moved to 109 Carlisle Road. In September of that year Tom married Tilly Cripps at Christ Church, Pitsmoor. The following year Millie and ten years later Olive were born to the couple. The Merrick family lived at 49 Hunsley Street, nearly opposite Hunsley Street Chapel, for many years.

On 17th July 1892 Joseph and Kate completed their family with the birth of Ernest, their only surviving son at 65 Hunsley Street.

As soon as he was old enough to make his own way across the street Ernest made friends with the neighbouring children. Across the road at 50 Hunsley Street lived the Alvey family. William Alvey was a Midland driver from Little Eaton in Derbyshire. Harry, William's eldest child, and Ernest became life-long friends.

Upon attaining school age Ernest and Harry entered Grimesthorpe Board Infants School where they were placed in the same class. On 25th March 1898 the Sheffield School Board presented Ernest with Alma Strettell's book – 'Lullabies of Many Lands' as a reward for punctual attendance. In 1900 Ernest received 'Yule-Tide Yarns' by G.A. Henty, a First Class Reward also for punctual attendance. Ernest enjoyed reading and Howard Robinson later recalled enjoyed reading his uncle's copy of 'The Last of the Mohicans'.

On Sunday afternoons Ernest and his sister Nellie attended the All Saints Church of England Sunday School. Afterwards they joined the other children at play in the street. One of their games was cherry bobs – knocking a cherry stone up a rainwater down-pipe with the flat of the hand and seeing how far its fall would propel it along the channel that crossed the pavement.

In 1899 a rag and bone merchant regularly disturbed the tranquillity of Hunsley Street with his loud horn. This was particularly thoughtless since many of the street's residents were railway employees and, of those, a fair proportion would be working nights and in need of their sleep during the daytime. It must have come as a relief to many when a policeman caught up with the offender.

The 1901 census indicates that a thirty-year-old railway engine fireman, Ernest Goodwin, lodged with the Craddock family at that time. An article published in the *Sheffield Daily Telegraph* of 30th December 1903 provides a glimpse of Joseph's life that would otherwise have been lost.

The previous Monday evening Joseph had chaired a social event organised by the Midland Railway Locomotive Benevolent Fund at the Old Green Dragon public house in Attercliffe. John Mason made a speech and then presented a smokers' cabinet to the head of the repairing staff at the engine shed at Millhouses for his efforts on behalf of the fund since he was leaving due to promotion to the locomotive shops at Derby. Tom Merrick was also present on the occasion which was followed by songs and recitations and a banjo solo and rounded off by Auld Lang Syne.

From 1903 to 1906 Ernest's future brother-in-law, William Henry Robinson, was a member of staff at Grimesthorpe Board School. Just before he left the Boys' Department, in March 1904, Ernest and three other boys were presented with prizes for their participation in the Sheffield Children's Hyacinth Show.

Later that year, Ernest and Harry Alvey entered Owler Lane Council School. At around that time Ernest displayed a flare for business. Having bought three identical newspapers for a penny he quickly sold two to break even but became a little concerned when the third paper was slow to sell.

Clearly, having an entrepreneurial zeal, when Ernest left school in 1906 he found himself a job with James Willis Nicholson of Plumpton, Ecclesall, a partner of Francis Ebenezer Smith, stock and share broker. For Ernest's father, who had benefited greatly from his career on the railway, trading in stocks and shares was beyond his knowledge and experience. As a result, Joseph insisted that his son give up his job and secure a trade apprenticeship. Ernest duly became an apprentice fitter in the electrical department at Vickers, Son & Maxim. At the same time Harry Alvey started work in the drawing office at Charles Cammell's.

Both Ernest and Harry continued their education at the Owler Lane Evening School and in July 1908 Harry gained first class and Ernest second class in the first year experimental mathematic course.

Both boys enjoyed cricket and in June that year they played for the Grimesthorpe U.M.C. against Newhall Primitives on Blackburn Meadows. The match ended in a tie with Ernest not out. In May 1909 they played for the same team against St. Clements' at Meadow Hall. Harry was run out and Ernest again not out.

The pair were also keen cyclists and toured the countryside with their friends. A faded photograph of Ernest, Harry Alvey, Tom Butterworth and Oswald Bunn with their bicycles at Mortomley in 1909 has been preserved. Mortomley adjoins High Green which is about eight miles north of Sheffield. (Harry later married Oswald Bunn's sister, Nora.)

Ernest and Harry cycled to Worcester on two occasions to spend fortnight holidays with Harry's aunt. On the first occasion they left home at three in the morning, stopped off at Derby to have breakfast with another of Harry's aunts, and arrived at Worcester at six in the evening. The pleasure of the virtually traffic-free roads would have been tempered by the poor road surfaces. Whilst their cycles were perhaps the fastest vehicles the boys encountered on their journeys, their fathers drove the fastest vehicles then devised by man.

Grimesthorpe United Methodist Free Church, Sheffield

known as Hunsley Street Chapel

Ernest Craddock, Harry Alvey, Tom Butterworth & Oswald Bunn

at Mortomley, 1909

CHAPTER NINE

Earl Marshal Road

At the dawn of the twentieth century Joseph Craddock and his family in Sheffield were removed, in more than location, from the family he had left in Kettering thirty years earlier. Joseph was one of the Midland Railway Company's nearly four thousand drivers who had reached the apex of working class affluence.

In 1903 Joseph filed his last will and testament and thus became the first member of his family line to do so. Everything was to be left to Kate with the exception of his watch and chain that were to go to Ernest when he reached the age of sixteen. Catherine Craddock and Alfred Thomas Wood were appointed executors and the will was witnessed by the latter and Jane Lucy Wood. They were a retired schoolmaster and his wife of Little Eaton in Derbyshire.

Whilst Ernest Craddock and Harry Alvey attended Owler Lane School, Harry's family left 50 Hunsley Street for Hamilton Road. Next door to the Alvey's old house, 48 Hunsley Street, lived John Trickett and his family.

Early in the twentieth century John Trickett made the transition from being a machine file cutter to an insurance agent for the Liverpool Victoria Insurance Corporation. The increased prosperity associated with his change in career enabled John and his family to move to 364 Earl Marshal Road – a road that was then sparsely built upon and surrounded by fields. Whilst the Craddock family were also contemplating a move, John Trickett's action appears to have helped their decision that Earl Marshal Road should be their destination.

Earl Marshal Road runs just to the north of Pitsmoor between Crabtree and Grimesthorpe. Although it was open to public traffic, it was a private road owned by the Duke of Norfolk's estate and had a five-barred gate halfway along its length that had to be opened every time a vehicle passed.

On 16th June 1908 Joseph paid Arthur Drew, a builder of 2 Norwood Road, Sheffield, a twenty pound deposit for the construction of two adjoining houses in Earl Marshal Road. The full cost was to be £430. Each house was to have two cellars, a living room, parlour, scullery, two bedrooms, bathroom, attic and an external water closet. The water closets and the chimney pots were to be modelled on those at 364 Earl Marshal Road. Indeed, since the builder's contract stated that John Trickett as well as Joseph and the City authorities were to be satisfied with the work, it is evident that John Trickett was of considerable assistance to Joseph. Perhaps by way of gratitude, Joseph later took out a £100 house contents insurance policy with the Liverpool Victoria Insurance Corporation.

The houses had a passage between them that led to back gardens that offered a splendid view over Wincobank. The front doors were opposite each other halfway along the passage that gave shelter like a porch. The parlour was at the front of the house, the living room behind, and a tiny scullery at the back with a sink.

It is stated in the builder's contract that Joseph would provide ranges and baths for both houses, which were to be installed by the builder. Those Joseph purchased from W.H. Micklethwait & Co. of Clough Works in Rotherham on 24th September 1908. The invoices list two ranges, numerous tiles, mantelpieces and two baths.

The houses were then nearing completion, since four days later Henry Webster, Architect and Valuer, valued the properties at £480 with a safe mortgage security of £320. On 1st October Joseph paid the builder a further £155 and Joseph's solicitor, William E. Dyson of Bingley & Dyson, witnessed the agreement. The remaining sum was to be paid upon completion of the purchase. To this end, in February 1909, an indenture was issued between the trustees of ASLEF, Moses John Dickinson and Richard Thomas Hatton, who were both Leeds engine drivers, and Joseph Craddock for a loan of £250.

Upon completion of the houses the Craddock family moved into 407 Earl Marshal Road and no. 405 was rented to the Stone family for 18s per week.

The Stone family had lived at 60 Newhall Road close to Grimesthorpe engine shed. Richard Stone left the Midland Railway soon after the turn of the century to run a coke-washing business. This involved buying waste material, sorting and re-selling it to the local steel works. Since Joseph had once served as Richard Stone's fireman, the families' new living arrangements represented a reversal of fortune. According to the 1911 census, Richard and his wife, Elizabeth, shared no. 405 with their adult children, Herbert and Lily.

At no. 407, where Edith and Nellie shared a bedroom, Ernest would have slept in the attic. However the latter's lasting memory of the new house was the improvement in lighting provided by the gas mantles in comparison to the old bats-wing burners at Hunsley Street.

Whilst the family lived in Hunsley Street Joseph had been accustomed to have the occasional drink with Tom Merrick and other friends in local public houses. However, after the move to Earl Marshal Road this activity became less convenient and subsequently less frequent.

In March 1909 a three-day bazaar was held at Hunsley Street Chapel with the objective of raising £150. Charles Wardlow, a steel manufacturer, opened the proceedings with the down-beat utterance that 'if there is any slumdom in Sheffield it is at Grimesthorpe'. Kate and her elder daughter Edith helped tend the Ladies' Congregational Stall whilst Nellie was at the Crockery Stall. Ernest and his friend Harry Alvey and others manned the Bazaar Room Entertainments.

In June of the following year the Chapel financial secretary, Willie Robinson, declared that they had wiped out the large debt. He was also the organising secretary of the Chapel Young People's Union of more than fifty members. A Miss Baxter and Edith were elected the Union representatives. Early in the century Edith had attended the Pupil Teachers' Centre in Holly Street where Willie Robinson was a fellow pupil.

William Henry Robinson was the son of Charles Christopher and Ann Robinson who arrived in Sheffield from Leake in Lincolnshire in the 1870s. Having trained at the Sheffield Training College in Collegiate Crescent and at Sheffield University, Willie Robinson embarked on a teaching career that would eventually lead to a headship.

Edith however, could not set her sights so high. In August 1904 she was transferred from Wincobank School to Carlisle Street but was sent to Newhall Junior instead! There she was placed in charge of the Standard I (d) class. Less than a year later the head teacher took Edith's class as she prepared for, and then sat, her certificate exam. Success in that meant promotion to the Standard I (b) class with sixty-one pupils under her charge. The following years however, proved to be demanding for Edith as she struggled with her own absences due to illness and the Standard II classes. In September 1911 her class was considered to be so backward that it was necessary for the head teacher to take part of it. Then, on 24th May 1912, the School closed at noon for the Whitsuntide vacation and Edith terminated her engagement as she was to be married five days later.

Edith Craddock and Willie Robinson were married on 29th May 1912 at Hunsley Street Chapel. Nellie's young man Bert Unwin was the best man, and Nellie and Willie's sister, Annie, were the bridesmaids. Willie had to get permission from the Duke of Norfolk's estate to have the five-bar gate situated halfway along Earl Marshal Road opened to allow the wedding party to pass. After the ceremony, guests were entertained at no. 407 where the newlyweds received gifts from family, friends and the Newhall and Grimethorpe schools. The wedding photograph taken in the back garden is noteworthy for the solemn expressions of the day and the central and dominant position of Willie's sister. The couple then departed for their honeymoon in Derbyshire.

During the period 1907-9 accidents on the railways were frequent and enginemen were punished for incidents that were outside of their control. This resulted, on 18th August 1911, in Britain's first national railway strike when virtually the whole country was brought to a standstill. Two days later, after costing ASLEF £2,561, the strike was over and a Royal Commission was set up to investigate the grievances.

In May 1912 Joseph attained his sixty-fifth birthday. In following years this birthday often marked the commencement of retirement. However, at that time no such rule applied and engine drivers could remain in service as long as they were able. Since only three years had passed since he commenced his ASLEF mortgage Joseph could not afford to give up work.

In the absence of documentary evidence or family recollections, the relationship between Joseph and his son, Ernest, early in the twentieth century can now only be imagined.

Joseph's responsible and demanding job, in terms of both time and energy, must have limited many of the usual father/son activities. Also, the forty-five year age gap and Joseph's limited world view beyond that of the railway must have presented obstacles. Joseph's intervention in his son's early working life and subsequent events may have initiated Ernest's desire to strike out on his own once he had reached the age of twenty-one. This may have resulted in Ernest living in accommodation away from Earl Marshal Road early in 1914. What is known for certain is that he joined 'A' Squadron of the Queen's Own Yorkshire Dragoons on 21st February 1914.

At Vickers, Ernest was acquainted with Matt Sheppard who had long been involved with the Territorial Force which after the 1908 army reforms became the Territorial Army.

Born in 1873, Matt Sheppard joined the Imperial Yeomanry in 1900 and saw active service in South Africa. Early in the new century Matt re-joined the Queen's Own Yorkshire Dragoons and, as he rose through the non-commissioned ranks, became a valuable recruiting sergeant for the regiment.

For Ernest, the attraction would have been the camaraderie associated with being a member of the regiment and an escape from work and parental restrictions. He would have learned that the 1914 Whitsuntide annual training camp was to take place at Scarborough and must have eagerly anticipated the event.

On 30th May 'A' Squadron paraded outside the Great Central Railway station (later named the Victoria station) in Sheffield when they were inspected by Lieutenant D.C. Leng. A photograph was taken of a group including Ernest and Squadron Sergeant-Major Matt Sheppard all looking very happy to be heading for the seaside.

At the camp, the regiment, under the command of Major W. McKenzie Smith, took part in a musketry course at Scalby Beck, mounted drill on Scarborough racecourse and field days in the countryside. On 4th June they were inspected by the Director-General of the Territorial Army and four days later by the General Officer in Command of the Northern Command. For generals and troopers alike the possibility of a major European war two months hence must have appeared quite remote.

For Joseph, the declaration of war on 4th August 1914 raised concerns for his son who was already in uniform, and for himself working on a railway under government control. At midnight that day the Railway Executive Committee took control of one hundred and thirty railway companies. Aside from a 60 mph speed restriction, state control had little impact on the running of individual companies.

A comprehensive account of Ernest's Great War service can be found in his older son's biography and a shorter account in a chapter in the second edition of this book. For those reasons it will not be repeated here.

The major events in the Craddock family during the Great War were the birth of Joseph and Kate's first grandchild, Nellie's marriage to Bert Unwin and Ernest's engagement to May Rideout.

Edith and Willie Robinson's first child, Howard, was born at 101 Scott Road in Pitsmoor on 30th March 1915. Two years later the family moved to 268 Ellesmere Road, next door to the shop that was run by Willie's parents and sister.

Nellie lived with her parents at 407 Earl Marshal Road whilst she earned a modest living by dressmaking. On 24th July 1915 she married Bert Unwin, a steel annealer, who was then lodging with the Robinson family at Scott Road. May Rideout was one of the bridesmaids so Ernest, who was then on the continent, was particularly disappointed to be unable to attend. After their marriage Nellie and Bert lived at 51 Idsworth Road. Bert played hockey on Saturday afternoons and in about 1920 he and Ernest made Howard Robinson a pedal car for Christmas.

Victoria May Rideout was so named because she was born on the day when Queen Victoria visited Sheffield in her diamond jubilee year, Friday 21st May 1897. May was the only surviving child of Henry Rideout, a coal merchant, and his wife Emily of 170 Scott Road, Pitsmoor.

Ernest took dancing lessons at Thomas Dey's Tower Ballroom on Pitsmoor Road. There, one Friday night in 1913 he met the sixteen-year-old May Rideout who was attracted to the boy with the 'dreamy eyes'. In the spring of 1917, when Ernest was home on leave, he asked Henry Rideout for his daughter's hand in marriage. In a letter to May written when he had returned to the continent, Ernest told her 'your father is fine & I shall make a good friend of him'.

Just over a year later, Ernest ended a letter to May with a post-script 'Shall I bring you a German helmet back?' Encumbered with the bulky souvenir, Ernest removed and kept the eagle badge and disposed of the helmet.

In November 1918 May contracted influenza. That year the so-called Spanish strain of the disease had ravaged the world and between September and November nearly a quarter of a million people died of flu in Britain. Since May was then considered to be a part of the family in all but name Joseph, who was concerned about her condition, wrote her a letter on 1st December.

Being on night duty Joseph had spent the greater part of the day in bed. In the evening Nellie and Bert went to chapel, Kate, having a bad cold, settled in an armchair and Mrs. Gascoyne wrote a letter to her husband in France. They were expecting their lodger, Percy Barrand, on Tuesday to stay the night and Gladys on Wednesday. Later in the evening Nellie and Bert returned with Ernest and Lizzie Kemble. Joseph conveyed the latter's regards to May in a post-script which was supplemented by both Nellie and Bert.

Percy Barrand came from Loughborough where he worked for the Brush Electric Company. The Sheffield trams had Brush electrical components and Percy worked in Sheffield in connection with the tramways. The Kembles lived in Upwell Street and were members of Hunsley Street Chapel.

In February 1919ASLEF agreed to the eight hour working day and the 48 hour week. Then, in the spring, the union signed an agreement that transferred part of an engine driver's, fireman's and cleaner's war wage to their permanent wage. This resulted in the publication of the first National Standardised Wages for British Enginemen. Other grades then demanded that all of their war wage should be transferred to their permanent wage. After failing to reach an agreement with the Government the National Executive of the National Union of Railwaymen (NUR) instructed its members to leave their posts. The ASLEF leadership then called out its own members in sympathy with the NUR. The result was a strike from 26th September.

Joseph, Tom Merrick and Tom's stepson-in-law, Percy Leach, who were all Midland enginemen and ASLEF members, withdrew their labour. However, for Joseph, a member of Sheffield No. 1 Branch, who had drawn between 6/8 and £3 6/8 per annum in sickness benefit since 1905 and was then in his seventy-third year, the strike marked the end of his 48½ year career with the Midland Railway Company.

Joseph then turned his attention to his family and home at 407 Earl Marshal Road. It is from this period that memories of Joseph by those who remember him have been recorded. Harry Alvey remembered Joseph as being a very quiet man. Olive French described her uncle as a gentleman who was perhaps overly influenced by his wife and daughters. As a young boy, Howard Robinson remembered his grandfather as tall and taciturn with closely cropped hair and a grey moustache. He recalled him sitting in an armchair between the fireplace and the window with Jimmy the canary in a brass cage almost overhead.

Ernest Craddock and May Rideout were married at St. James' Presbyterian Church on Scott Road on 2nd June 1920. Percy Barrand was the best man, Laura Bagshaw, the matron of honour, and May's young cousins, Joyce Fletcher and Margaret Draper, the bridesmaids. The horse-drawn carriages were provided by John Heath's firm.

During the reception, which was held at Dey's Tower Ballroom on Pitsmoor Road, May's uncle, Arthur Rideout, who was a professional photographer, took a splendid group photograph of the couple surrounded by their families. The send off, with decorations attached to the back of the taxi, was matched by that at the station as the couple was sent on their way to their honeymoon in Llandudno.

After the nuptials Ernest and May spent three months living with May's parents at 170 Scott Road before moving into one of the first council houses, 52 Edensor Road on the Norwood estate. It was at that address that their first child was born on 12th April 1921. At May's mother's request, the boy was christened Stanley Rideout Craddock in memory of his uncle, Stanley Hazell Rideout, who had died as an infant of pneumonia in 1901.

When Stanley was three months old the young family spent an enjoyable fortnight in Southport, the guest of May's widowed aunt Ada Hazell.

During the spring or summer of 1921 Sylvia Kennedy of Melbourne in Australia paid a visit to Sheffield. Edith with baby Margaret (always known as Peggy) met Howard at Firs Hill School and they went to Roe Woods with Joseph, Kate and Sylvia where they enjoyed a picnic. There Edith took a photograph of her parents with 'Cousin Syl'. That photograph and memory of the visit is important for this family history since it is the only evidence that Joseph kept in touch with his family in Kettering. After that event contact was gradually lost but not irretrievably broken.

After their afternoon Sunday school attendance, Howard and Peggy would visit 407 Earl Marshal Road where they collected caterpillars from their grandfather's cabbages whilst their mother helped prepare tea. After the meal the family, except for Joseph, returned to Hunsley Street Chapel with their neighbour Elizabeth Stone for the six o'clock service. Invariably they were a few minutes late.

The years 1923 and 1924 brought three deaths to 407 Earl Marshal Road.

During the last two days of June 1923 Nellie and Bert Unwin's baby daughter, Betty, spent her short life in the house.

In 1924 Joseph visited Fir Vale Hospital on 4th and 11th April concerning an intestinal obstruction. On 26th of that month he entered the hospital and returned home on 1ˢᵗ May. According to Olive French, on the morning of 6ᵗʰ May her father, Tom Merrick, called at the public house at the top of Hunsley Street to buy a drink for his brother-in-law. Later that day Joseph died of heart failure aged nearly seventy-seven.

Elizabeth Stone laid out Joseph's body and it remained in the parlour for three days. After a short service at home, at 2pm on 9ᵗʰ May Joseph was laid to rest at St. Thomas's Church in Brightside.

In his will Joseph left £1,312 gross (£1,287 net), a fair sum considering his poor start in life. His watch and chain should have been left to Ernest but only the 9 carat gold chain and bar with an Albert fashioned from a George IV 1826 shilling was passed to Ernest's younger son.

Soon after her father's death, Nellie became critically ill with peritonitis and Edith, Howard and Peggy moved to 407 Earl Marshal Road so that Edith could help her mother nurse her sister. Unfortunately, it was to no avail and Nellie died on 30ᵗʰ June 1924, a year to the day after the death of her only child. Nellie was only in her thirty-fifth year.

Kate received support in her grief from her surviving children, Edith and Ernest, and their families. She and Elizabeth Stone kept each other company and took turns to buy an evening newspaper. Kate continued to live at 407 Earl Marshal Road until the late 1920s when illness compelled her to move in with the Robinson family at 268 Ellesmere Road.

There Kate remained virtually bed-bound until she died in December 1932. Howard was despatched by bicycle to inform the Merrick family at 49 Hunsley Street. In that small house lived Tilly and Tom Merrick, their daughter Olive and Tilly's daughter Hetty and her husband Percy Leach. The family had a large white Pomeranian dog called Bobs: named after Field Marshal Lord Roberts of Boer War fame.

After Kate left 407 Earl Marshal Road the house was rented to her niece, Millie Dobson, and her family until about 1936. Millie's husband, Abraham Fearnley Dobson, known as Harry, established a successful hardware business. After the departure of the Dobson family no. 407 was occupied by members of the Levick family until the 1970s. Ernest, and later his elder son, Stanley, collected the rent from the property until 407 Earl Marshal Road was sold to Jeffrey Rhodes in 1976. (The latter had been taught by Stanley Craddock at Owler Lane School.)

Edith Craddock & Willie Robinson's wedding, 29th May 1912

the back garden of 407 Earl Marshal Road, Sheffield

Nellie Craddock & Bert Unwin's wedding, 24th July 1915

standing on the right are May Rideout & Percy Barrard

Kate & Joseph Craddock with Syl Kennedy from Melbourne, Australia

Roe Woods, Sheffield, 1921

Joseph, Stanley & Ernest Craddock, circa 1923

CHAPTER TEN

'The Business'

On Monday, 27th January 1919, after his army service in the Great War, Ernest recommenced work as a fitter at Vickers, Son & Maxim in Sheffield. During his first week he was put onto repairs to ease him into the swing of things. Unfortunately, there was an unpleasant atmosphere at the works. There was the threat of strikes and men who had stayed at home on war work boasted of their earnings during the conflict.

After his marriage and much deliberation, Ernest decided to accept his father-in-law Henry Rideout's offer of a partnership in his coal merchant business. May, however, was not so keen. She knew that 'the business', as she called it, had little working capital and that before her marriage she had often been asked to take money to the bank so that a cheque could be honoured. She was pretty sure that the money that Ernest brought to the business was virtually all there was.

Ernest was the mainstay from the start and during his first few months he cycled the hilly route from 52 Edensor Road to 170 Scott Road each day. Henry Rideout had used a flat-topped dray for hundredweight sacks and a tipping cart for loose coal – both horse drawn – and he never used a motor lorry. In November 1921 Ernest sold Tommy the horse and the carts and from then on he relied on his Ford Model T lorry. The vehicle had been imported from the U.S.A. and so had a left hand drive. Howard Robinson used to hang about the yard in the school holidays in the hope that his uncle would give him a ride.

During the following years Henry Rideout suffered from rheumatoid arthritis which was then known as progressive paralysis. This severely eroded his contribution to the business and made Ernest not only responsible for his growing family but also for his parents-in-law.

To be closer to the business, in 1923, Ernest, May and Stanley moved to 164 Scott Road where Joan Hazel Craddock was born on 23rd December. The following year Ernest attended a service at Hunsley Street chapel when May discovered that he had left his best bowler hat at home. Concerned that Ernest had gone off in the old brown bowler that he gave Stanley to play with, May put Joan in the pram and hurried to the chapel to swap her husband's headwear.

During the General Strike of May 1926 when coal was rationed, Ernest augmented his supplies at a coal outcrop at Troway.

Around 1927 the Ford lorry was superseded by a Dennis with solid tyres. With help from Hornbuckles, monumental masons of Malton Street, Ernest built a garage for the lorry behind 170 Scott Road with materials purchased from the demolition of Coal Aston Aerodrome on the outskirts of Sheffield. Then, when Mrs. Driver, the Rideout's tenant at 168 Scott Road left, the Craddock family moved next door to Henry and Emily.

Since the business required regular deliveries, Ernest felt that he could not afford the time for holidays and he did not have what was considered to be a proper one for twenty-four years. However, he took his family on holiday, and stayed a night or two before returning to Sheffield, and collected them a week later. The family stayed in boarding houses in Bridlington and Scarborough. They also went to Cleethorpes and Theddlethorpe on one occasion each.

In the summer of 1929 Stanley and Joan went on holiday to Bridlington with their aunt and uncle, Edith and Willie Robinson, and their children, Howard and Peggy. When they returned home they found they had a baby brother, Peter Ernest Craddock, born at 168 Scott Road on 3rd September.

Despite the pride and freedom associated with having his own business, Ernest had embarked on a life of unremitting physical hard work.

Having received a note informing him that his coal would be available on a particular date, Ernest and his employee would drive to the Midland Railway goods Wicker Station off Savile Street to look for their wagon. Ernest would then draw the lorry next to the wagon and whilst the wagon door was supported by his mate's shoulders the catches were knocked-up with an ash pole. The door would then be lowered as the coal spilled out on to the bed of the lorry. There was then the laborious two-man job of shovelling the entire contents of the wagon into bags. As each was filled it was lifted on to the scales for weighing.

Ernest was a precise man and his younger son remembered the occasion when his adjustment of the contents of a sack by adding or removing a lump of coal caused some amusement to fellow workers engaged in the same activity. The point was that Ernest was dealing with his own coal and he neither wanted to give coal away nor supply his customers with a short measure. The other workers were, no doubt, employed by a large firm and unconcerned by such niceties. At the time when the Sheffield gangs were active, Ernest had to stand his ground and see off a pair of thugs intent on stealing his coal.

With the coal bagged and weighed it would then be delivered to his customers. For the work of carrying the bags Ernest would wear a leather protector on his back. Deliveries were usually done by tipping the contents of bags down the coal grate (at the front or side of the house) into the coal cellar. The empty bags would then be stacked on the lorry as a check of the quantity delivered. Larger quantities of coal were delivered loose by shovelling directly down the grate. As a small boy Peter helped his father with this work using his seaside spade.

After a day's deliveries Ernest would spend the evening seated at the bureau at home writing out bills from his notebook and keeping the business accounts. Ernest was constantly frustrated by professional people (and others with a regular income) who were slow to settle their bills. When Ernest was on his round May (or another member of the family) would deal with customers calling at the house. If there was a telephone call or a message for Ernest, May would put an envelope in the window as a signal for him to call. Since private telephones were quite rare in Pitsmoor in the 1930s, sometimes neighbours seeking the favour of using the phone were charged 2d to make a call since May found the intrusion a nuisance.

At the end of a day's toil and a bath, Ernest's youngest child would sit on his knee and remove the tiny flecks of coal dust from the corners of his eyes.

When there were no collections or deliveries to be made Ernest would spend time making repairs. There were coal bags to be darned with a large curved needle and a ball of twine and the lorry bed (that received a lot of wear) to be reinforced. As a boy, Peter, playing with a large spanner, once over-tightened a nut on the lorry so stripping the thread resulting in the inevitable replacement work.

Around 1936 Ernest took delivery of a Bedford three-ton lorry. It displayed 'E. Craddock' on the cab door and 'The Best is the Cheapest' on the tailboard. Ernest also built three motorcycle garages to rent.

In the winter Ernest hung a coal fire from the lorry tailboard to thaw out frozen bags and his hands. The latter suffered from the arduous work of carrying bags of coal and chilblains and they became deeply cracked. He would remove the dirt with a sand and soft-soap compound and then soak them in warm water and rub in goose-grease for relief.

Ernest also used his Bedford lorry to develop a haulage side to the business. Charlie Bufton, Morton and Storer's manager, provided a lot of work for Ernest transporting limestone from Derbyshire quarries. At Whitsuntide the lorry was given a thorough spring-clean and used to transport people, equipment and food to Firth Park for the annual celebration.

Ernest bought his first car in 1932 which was garaged in the old stables. It was a 1924 Austin open tourer. Private cars were quite rare in the district so Ernest would occasionally hire his out to take people on holiday and collect them afterward. Ernest would also press his vehicle into service for weddings.

In November Ernest met up with Clarry Gilliat, a Great War 4th Troop comrade, at a Queen's Own Yorkshire Dragoon's Old Comrade's Association meeting. Clarry was a farmer and he and his family lived at Yew Tree Farm at Auckley near Doncaster and later at Mosham. The Craddock family enjoyed the delights of a proper mixed farm and the Gilliats' hospitality on many occasions.

Stanley and Joan attended Firs Hill School on Barnsley Road. When May, who had been an old pupil, took Peter to the school she was asked by a teacher 'What, another?' Stanley later attended Firth Park Grammar School, from which he matriculated with distinction, and was then employed by the mining machinery company Hardy Patent Pick.

Henry Rideout's health eventually declined to the point where he was confined to his bed in the downstairs front room and was cared for by his wife and daughter. A small Christmas tree was bought for him, which is still displayed each year. He died on 1st December 1937 aged just sixty-seven.

In the New Year it was decided that the Craddock family would move into 170 Scott Road with May's mother, Emily Rideout, and no. 168 was let. (No. 170 had the advantage of having an inside toilet.) The front room was Emily's sitting room, where Peter would take his grandmother her meals and occasionally play whist with her, so the rest of the family found the remainder of the house a little cramped. Ernest, May (and soon baby Anne) occupied the front bedroom, Joan and Emily the back bedroom and Stanley and Peter were in the attic. Naturally, neither Emily nor Joan was happy with the arrangement.

That summer Joan and Peter went on holiday to North Wales with the Robinson family and shortly after their return May gave birth to a baby girl at Marlcliffe Nursing Home. As a consolation for losing his position as the youngest member of the family, Peter was asked to choose the baby's name: Anne Patricia.

Ernest employed several men over the years to assist him with the business. There was Old Ernest, who had been called up towards the end of the Great War, and George, a large but simple man. On one occasion the two-year old Anne pinched George's sandwiches so he complained to May. During the war it was particularly difficult to get any sort of labour and Ernest was a regular visitor to the Labour Exchange. Unfortunately, the best applicant was the 'Duke of Darnall', a harmless but unemployable character who fantasised that he was a toff.

After the war Ernest had a help called Albert, then two lads including Fred who freed him from carrying the heavy bags of coal.

On Friday nights Ernest would return home with a bar of chocolate for everyone in the family that he had bought from a customer's sweet shop. After working on Saturday mornings he would rest in the afternoon. Although Ernest was a practical man he always employed local tradesmen to decorate the house in return for the trade they gave him and, in any case, May preferred him to rest.

Ernest in the left hand driving seat of his Ford Model T lorry, 1921

Joan, Stanley, Peter, May & Ernest, Scarborough, circa 1935

CHAPTER ELEVEN

The War

The approaching conflict with Germany was more evident to Stanley than the Great War had been to his father a quarter of a century earlier.

In 1938 Stanley went to the Royal Artillery drill hall at Middlewood with the intention of enlisting in the Territorial Army but he was deemed to be too young to join without his parents' permission. In the spring of the following year, as soon as he had turned eighteen, Stanley joined his father's old unit, 'A' Squadron, the Queen's Own Yorkshire Dragoons. He was with the regiment at their annual camp at Fourstones Park, Newbrough, near Hexham for a very hot Whitsuntide fortnight.

During the first half of September 'A' Squadron was based at Norbury Hall, the Drill Hall, off Barnsley Road. Then the whole regiment moved to various villages near Malton where they received their horses. 'A' Squadron was based at Hovingham where a few Great War veterans including Ernest and Captain Matt Sheppard visited them one weekend. They borrowed some of the fine Worcestershire hunters and Ernest had his first ride since 1918.

In Sheffield the family was provided with gas-masks. These were selected for fit to obtain the desired seal and contained in a cardboard box that had to be carried at all times. Baby Anne was provided with a version that enveloped the upper part of her body and was secured with a belt around her waist. Despite the plentiful provision of air that was supplied by means of a hand-operated pump, Anne made it perfectly clear what she thought of the apparatus.

With war imminent, May insisted that a professional photograph was taken of the four siblings. With Stanley in army uniform, May had a real fear, borne from her memory of so many male acquaintances lost in the Great War, that her oldest son might fail to return from the approaching conflict.

War with Germany was declared on 3rd September 1939, Peter's tenth birthday. That day Ernest and May took Joan and Peter to Darley Dale to stay with Ernest's cousin Ted Milner and his family. Peter was relieved to have avoided the fate of the majority of his Firs Hill school-mates who were evacuated to Mountsorrel in Leicestershire. That night the air-raid sirens sounded for the first time.

Back in Sheffield, Ernest's Bedford lorry was commandeered but it was not explained how halting a family business and depriving many homes of fuel would help the war effort. Ernest eventually managed to locate his lorry and retrieve it from the Fire Service.

Coal was put on ration and customers were obliged to register with a particular merchant. This had the desirable effect of reducing bad debts since such people no longer had the option of transferring to another source of supply.

At 'Dunholme' in Hackney, Darley Dale, Ted and Edie Milner and their daughters Peggy and Doreen welcomed the two Sheffield evacuees.

Being close in age, Peggy shared her bedroom with Joan while Doreen and Peter occupied the third bedroom. Since Doreen was then thirteen, the arrangement proved to be awkward for both her and Peter. Doreen particularly objected to Peter spitting in the bath – a reference to him cleaning his teeth using the bath when the basin was used by someone else.

Subject to the availability of sufficient petrol Ernest and May visited their children most weekends.

Peter attended the village school where there were a few fellow evacuees but he found his Derbyshire contemporaries to be lacking both his academic and social skills. Joan, who was then approaching sixteen, went to Matlock for shorthand and typing lessons which she did not enjoy.

During the period of the 'Phoney war' Peter returned to 'Dunholme' from school one day to discover that Joan had returned to Sheffield without mentioning it to him to avoid a possible difficult parting from her younger brother. Joan applied for and was accepted for a job in the photograph and print room at the English Steel Corporation where Ernest's life-long friend, Harry Alvey, was the chief engineer. Later, as a draughtswoman at the firm, Joan prepared drawings for Barnes Wallis' Tall Boy and other bombs.

Peter returned home in time for Christmas. It is believed that that was the year when 'Father Christmas' dropped a Meccano set no. 5 down the stairs. Despite most of Peter's schoolmates having returned to Sheffield, Firs Hill School remained closed and the Education Home Service was set up. That allowed children to be taught in small groups in private houses and so reduce the risk during an air raid. Firs Hill School was re-opened once its own shelters had been built.

Ernest's nephew, Howard Robinson, had a different view of the war.

Howard had attended Sheffield University and was elected President of the Student's Union in his final year. He then secured a position as an assistant master at Woodhouse Grove School, Apperley Bridge, Bradford.

In April 1940, when Howard had just turned twenty-five, he was required to register for military service but decided to declare himself a conscientious objector. His tribunal, which was held during the following month in Leeds, was reported in the Sheffield *Telegraph and Independent*. Howard stated that he objected to military service on Christian grounds and that by joining the forces he would be helping to carry on the war. He said that he thought his best service was to continue teaching. Judge Stewart replied with 'Piffle, and you must know it'.

Howard was registered for non-combatant service and called up on 1st June. In November Howard married Margaret Melluish and later that month he was commissioned into the York and Lancaster Regiment where he served in administrative roles for the remainder of the war.

Throughout the war a sign was displayed over the kitchen mantelpiece at 170 Scott Road. It read –

> There is no depression in this house, and we are not interested in the possibilities of defeat, they do not exist.

May put up black-out curtains and Ernest devised a mechanism that lowered a tin over the kitchen light whenever the outside door was opened. Ernest removed the rockery in the back yard, dug an enormous hole and erected an Anderson shelter with a blast wall in front of the door that he made by filling a bent steel sheet with soil and rubble. The shelter was provided with a sump and fitted with a plank floor, benches and a cupboard.

Being attracted to Joan, George Storer was a regular caller. One evening, during the black-out, May called out from the kitchen 'Come in George' only for George Walker, the young parson at St. James' Church, to enter. For May, who would never have dreamt of addressing a clergyman, however young, by his Christian name, the embarrassment of that greeting remained with her into old age.

Anne was an active little girl and 'into everything' including pulling a pile of Pyrex dishes from the sideboard. Several items were broken that were irreplaceable during the war. Then, on her second birthday, 18th August 1940, the air attacks on Sheffield started. That night Ernest, May, Joan, Peter and Anne shared their air-raid shelter with the Heginbotham family, the tenants of no. 168.

Later Ernest made a more comfortable and convenient shelter in the cellar by bricking up the ground-level window, reinforcing the ceiling and installing bunks. He also made an emergency exit through the cellar wall into the cellar of no. 168. The new tenants, Mr. & Mrs. Brown shared the shelter with the Craddock family and when there was no danger from enemy aircraft one of the adults would go upstairs to a kitchen to make a pot of tea.

Ernest did not join the Local Defence Volunteers (later renamed the Home Guard) due to what he perceived as the inherent snobbery based on position in civil life. However, he was a street warden and was on hand to help if needed. He was issued with a composition helmet and informed of the degree of air-raid alert. Ernest also acquired a stirrup pump for fire fighting and a sign to that effect was painted on their gate.

One of Peter's contributions to the war effort was to help his friends collect aluminium saucepans and take them in a barrow to the collection depot at the RAF barrage balloon base on Scott Road.

In late 1939 Stanley was with 'A' Squadron which was distributed over the Girsby Manor estate near the village of Ludford. When it became known that the regiment was to embark for the Middle East the family paid him a visit and enjoyed the spectacle of mounted men on exercise. Later it was declared that those under nineteen would not be permitted to serve abroad. Belonging in this category, on New Year's Day 1940, Stanley was transferred to a light Anti-Aircraft regiment of the Royal Artillery with H.Q. at Lincoln. For a short time he found himself posted to an A.A. installation on the outskirts of Sheffield. Later Stanley served with the First Army in North Africa, the Fifth Army in Italy and the 13th Infantry Division in Greece.

Early in 1940 Ernest bought an Austin 10 to economise on petrol. During the following year the petrol ration for private cars was removed but continued for motorcycles for another six months. In view of this, Ernest bought a Matchless 500 motorcycle that Stanley found particularly useful when he returned home on leave.

During the Sheffield Blitz of 12th and 13th December 1940 Ernest remained at 170 Scott Road whilst his family stayed with the Ward family at Birley Carr. (Fred Ward was the father of May's friend and matron of honour at her wedding, Laura

Bagshaw.) Stanley arrived home on leave the following day to find all the windows broken and soot blown down the chimney making the house temporarily uninhabitable.

On 11th October 1941 Stanley was again at home on leave when there was another air raid. Ernest was in the road on street duty. May, Joan and Peter went to the cellar whilst Stanley remained in the front room with Anne. Suddenly, a bomb dropped close by and Stanley just had time to shield his young sister as the blast hit the house sending soot down the chimney into the room. Five houses on Ellesmere Road and three on Kirton Road were demolished. May rushed in to take Anne, and Stanley went out into the street to find his father who was picking himself up from the ground. Ernest and Stanley then started to lift away the remains of a nearby house in which someone was still alive. Much to their annoyance, when the emergency services arrived, they were asked to move aside. Kenneth Middleton, a friend of Peter's age, who had been sheltering under the kitchen sink, was the only survivor of his family of four. Four members of the Tempest family next door were killed.

After that air raid the house was again temporarily uninhabitable. Following an offer from May's cousin, Douglas Woodcock, Peter spent a period with the Woodcock family in Bents Drive. Douglas Woodcock, his wife Myra and daughter Sonia lived next door to Douglas's parents, Tilly (nee Rideout) and George Arthur Woodcock, who had founded the firm Woodcock Travel in 1897.

After the shock of the air raid and having just started at the nearby High Storrs Grammar School, it was a difficult time for Peter. Despite residing within easy walking distance, he was occasionally late for school and received little sympathy from the teachers. In the evenings Peter and Sonia enjoyed playing the Lexicon word game. To add to their amusement, they would 'fix' the cards so that they could defeat Douglas when he joined in the game during the evening.

In 1942 Stanley returned home on leave to find his father in sole possession of the property. After the Blitz the family returned home but May's mother, Emily Rideout, took a bed-sitting room in Bridge End Farm at Derwent, a remote Derbyshire village. Peter visited his grandmother at Derwent on several occasions and he saw RAF bombers practising low level passes for what he later learned was the 'Dambusters' raid.

From that year the family, probably at May's instigation, owned a budgerigar which was named Cobber after the New Zealand air ace, 'Cobber' Kain. Old Cobber lived until 1949 when he was replaced by new Cobber, a Green Un' (after the Sheffield sporting newspaper).

Late in 1943, when Peter was fourteen and attending High Storrs Grammar School, his parents considered his future.

Ernest knew Charlie Bufton, the manager of Morton and Storer, through occasional work of transporting Derbyshire limestone for the company. Ernest and Charlie had similar values and became close friends. Through his work, Charlie became acquainted with the local Imperial Chemical Industries (ICI) representative, John Littler, and was impressed with his life-style and station in life. Charlie told Peter *'Get in with ICI lad and you're away'*. A new ICI office was to be opened in Sheffield early in the New Year and it became clear to Ernest that that was an ideal opportunity for his younger son.

Peter was not party to his parents' discussions concerning his future. Ernest and May did not want to take him out of school and they spent some sleepless nights discussing it. Stanley, away on active service, wrote to his parents stating his objection to the idea, however, the opportunity of a job with ICI proved irresistible. After a sum of money had been paid to release Peter from school he joined ICI in their office at 285 Glossop Road in March 1944 at the age of fourteen and a half.

Initially, Peter was the office junior with the job of dealing with the mail, however, since he took an interest in the activities of the office and evidently showed promise, in August 1945 he was promoted to order clerk. Having left school without a School Certificate, Peter enrolled at the Technical College night school in the old Central School to study five subjects and sit the exam extramurally.

Peter's interest in chemistry was initiated at High Storrs and given fresh impetus by his job in the chemical industry and the availability of (what would now be considered dangerous) chemicals in Sheffield. He had the attic bedroom to himself from where he conducted his often explosive experiments. This resulted in several loud reports and climaxed when he gave himself a fright with his home-made nitro-glycerine that had to be quickly disposed of down the toilet. Presumably under the impression that Peter's chemical experiments were part of his work, Ernest and May were very tolerant of their son's activities. Indeed, Ernest helped Peter fit out the loft over the garage into a proposed plastics factory.

As the War drew to a close, Ernest acquired an Austin five-ton lorry that required him to extend the garage.

Stanley returned home on 12th May 1946 fit, tanned and six foot three. As he and Peter once again shared the attic at 170 Scott Road they caught up with their very different experiences of the war. That summer the whole family went on holiday to Bournemouth, the only occasion when they were all present from beginning to end.

Joan, Peter, Anne & Stanley Craddock, 1939

Ernest, May, Peter, Stanley, Joan & Anne Craddock, circa 1940

CHAPTER TWELVE

Abbeyfield Road

The winter of 1946/7 was exceptionally severe and for a time Sheffield was cut off by road and rail. Ernest's services were in great demand but coal was in short supply. However, he did not want either of his sons to continue the business. It was hard, physical work and Ernest wanted them to pursue a profession.

On 20th November 1947, Princess Elizabeth's wedding day, Ernest's man failed to turn up so Stanley worked with his father that day. Ernest was reluctant but Stanley enjoyed the novelty. Later, when Ernest was ill he refused Peter's offer of help. Ernest had been known to continue to work through a bout of influenza. Such activity was likely to have caused permanent damage to his heart.

That year, having learned that a friend was considering training to be a school teacher, Stanley decided to join him and so he left the mining machinery company Hardy Patent Pick. Stanley trained at his Uncle Willie Robinson's old school, Pipworth Road, and commenced his career at Woodseats School on 1st March 1948. Willie, a career-long member and official of the National Union of Teachers was slightly miffed when Stanley joined the National Association of Schoolmasters but Stanley always insisted that he was a schoolmaster.

It never occurred to Peter to follow his father and brother into the army for his two year National Service. He thought that the RAF might provide a more interesting and comfortable existence. After ten days in Padgate near Warrington, the reception centre for the north, Peter spent eight weeks basic training at Innsworth near Gloucester. Towards the end of that period he was tested and asked what jobs (in order of priority) he would like to do. With an aptitude for Morse code and with the RAF's requirement for Radio Operators, Peter was sent on an eight-month course where he learnt to transmit and receive Morse with both speed and precision.

With RAF bombers flying training sorties over the Wash it was necessary for rescue launches to patrol in the event of an aircraft being forced to ditch. For several months Peter was the wireless operator on board one such launch.

On 4th September 1948 Joan married Philip Wade at St. James' Church on Scott Road. The reception was held at St. Cuthbert's Church hall. Daunted at the prospect of making a speech as the father of the bride, Ernest asked his brother-in-law, Willie Robinson, to speak in his stead. After the nuptials the couple lived in rented rooms at 745 Ecclesall Road, then at 170 Scott Road before moving to 22 Conalan Avenue in Bradway.

Tragedy struck the family ten days before Christmas when Ernest's sister, Edith Robinson, who had suffered a stroke, died aged sixty-five. Anne recalled that it was the only occasion she had seen her father weep.

In summer of 1949 the Craddock family left 170 Scott Road for a bay-windowed semi-detached villa with garage, 278 Abbeyfield Road. Under Ernest's direction, Peter lowered a wardrobe out of the Scott Road attic window to Stanley who was standing on a ladder that rested on the bed of the lorry. Around the time of the move Jill, a pedigree Scottie, was acquired for Anne.

After his two years of National Service Peter was transferred to the reserve and re-joined ICI. In order to catch up on his education he was sent to Bolton Technical College for a few weeks with a group of young men from ICI and BP.

Peter's life alternated between living with his parents at 278 Abbeyfield Road whilst working at the ICI offices in Sheffield and working in Manchester. The latter meant a long day commuting by rail though later Peter obtained digs in Manchester.

On 12th August 1950 Stanley married Eileen Hall at St. Cuthbert's Church.

In 1951 during the Korean War, reservists such as Peter were recalled to the services to replace those who had been sent to the Far East. After only a fortnight of additional service Peter was allowed to return to civilian life.

There was a strange occurrence during the Craddock family's first year in Abbeyfield Road.

May was acquainted with the elderly Miss Elizabeth Russell who had been employed as a cleaner by various members of her family. May occasionally carried her shopping home for her but never called upon her cleaning services. Miss Russell was an odd character whose tiny unkempt house at 5 Stockton Street had no electricity and relied on a street lamp for illumination.

After Miss Russell suffered a fall, May visited her in hospital and to alleviate the old ladies' worry agreed to fetch the money from her house. Having done so, Miss Russell became agitated and insisted that there was more. Indeed there was; gold sovereigns and half-sovereigns bursting from rotten bags which were counted on the dining room table behind closed curtains at Abbeyfield Road.

After Miss Russell died in July, May discovered that she was the sole executor of her will. That required her to communicate with members of Miss Russell's family including a nephew, Stanley Woodward, who visited from London. Her family agreed that Miss Russell had been foolish to live as she did whilst in possession of such wealth but she had insisted that it was 'family money' that could not be touched.

Acting on advice from her bank, May went to the Sheffield Smelting Company where there was someone she knew and could help her deal with the near two thousand pounds worth of coins.

Later, at 278 Abbeyfield Road, May's mother, Emily Rideout, took to her bed as an elderly invalid. She occupied the front ground floor room and had a bell with which she could summon assistance.

In the middle of one particular night the bell rang and Emily told May that someone had been in her room. Upon investigating May discovered that they had forgotten to lock the kitchen door. She locked the door, bolted the scullery door and returned to bed. Emily died in the house on 21st June 1955.

Peter worked at the ICI office in Glossop Road in Sheffield. During lunchtime walks with colleagues Peter noticed a group of girls doing likewise. They were typists of Hulse & Waite, Chartered Patent Agents, which included Kay Hulse, the younger daughter of the senior partner.

In December 1954 Peter went to a dance at Nether Edge Hall where Kay Hulse was also present. On seeing Peter, Kay asked one of her friends to change seats with her so that Peter could more easily see her and so ask for a dance.

On New Year's Day 1955 Kay introduced Peter to her family at 'Woodlands', 232 Abbeydale Road South, opposite Dore & Totley railway station. It was then a full household for as well as Mr. & Mrs. Hulse, Mrs. Hulse's father, Kay's sister Enid, her husband Les and their young son Robert, and Kay's brother Bill all resided in the large Victorian villa.

Later that year Peter's job again took him back to Manchester. As his train steamed through Dore & Totley station Kay waved from the attic window of her bedroom at 'Woodlands'.

On 1st October Kay celebrated both her twenty-third birthday and her engagement to Peter. Always one for having things done properly, Kay insisted that Peter propose on one knee.

Peter Craddock and Katharine Hulse were married on 16th June 1956 at St. John's Church, Abbeydale. Stanley was the best man and Kay's friend, Barbara Thompson, the chief bridesmaid. The other bridesmaids were Anne Craddock and Janet Macdonald, Bill Hulse's fiancé.

Peter and Kay spent their first night of married life in Stratford-upon-Avon followed by a fortnight in Swanage. They travelled from there by bus and boat along the coast.

After the nuptials the couple went to Manchester to stay with Peter's old landlady Mrs. Jenkinson at 15 Omer Drive in Burnage. The accommodation was basic and they knew what meal would be on offer from the day of the week, but they were lucky to find a landlady prepared to take in a married couple. Kay found a job as a typist in the city and together Peter and Kay travelled to and fro on the bus whilst their house was being built in Heald Green.

Ernest was diagnosed with angina in 1954 but that did not discourage him from buying a new model Austin A50 during the following year.

In July 1955 he, May and Anne went on a coach tour to Paris, Brussels and Le Touquet. Ignoring his wife and daughter's advice not to, Ernest tried out a few of the phases of French he had picked up during the Great War forty years before.

Anne's dog, Jill, died in September 1956 and was replaced the next month by May's selection of a Scottie bitch puppy called Judy.

In 1957, having reached his sixty-fifth birthday, Ernest sold the coal merchant business and retired. The final weekend was very busy. Ernest and May had their granddaughter three-year old Susan Wade staying with them and people had been coming and going to settle their bills. May occasionally left her rings lying around in the kitchen but then she discovered that they were missing. The police were called and a detective asked May if she could pick out anyone from their list of clients. May refused to speculate and Ernest persuaded her to accept the loss. What May could not understand was that she considered Judy to be a good house dog and concluded that she must have known the thief.

In August 1958 Ernest, May and Anne moved into a bungalow, 14 Hemper Lane in Bradway. Their new home had large front and back gardens and was directly across the road from Stanley, Eileen and baby James.

Joan Craddock & Philip Wade's wedding, 4th September 1948
St. James' Church, Scott Road, Sheffield

Ernest & May Craddock's ruby wedding celebration, 4th June 1960
14 Hemper Lane, Bradway, Sheffield

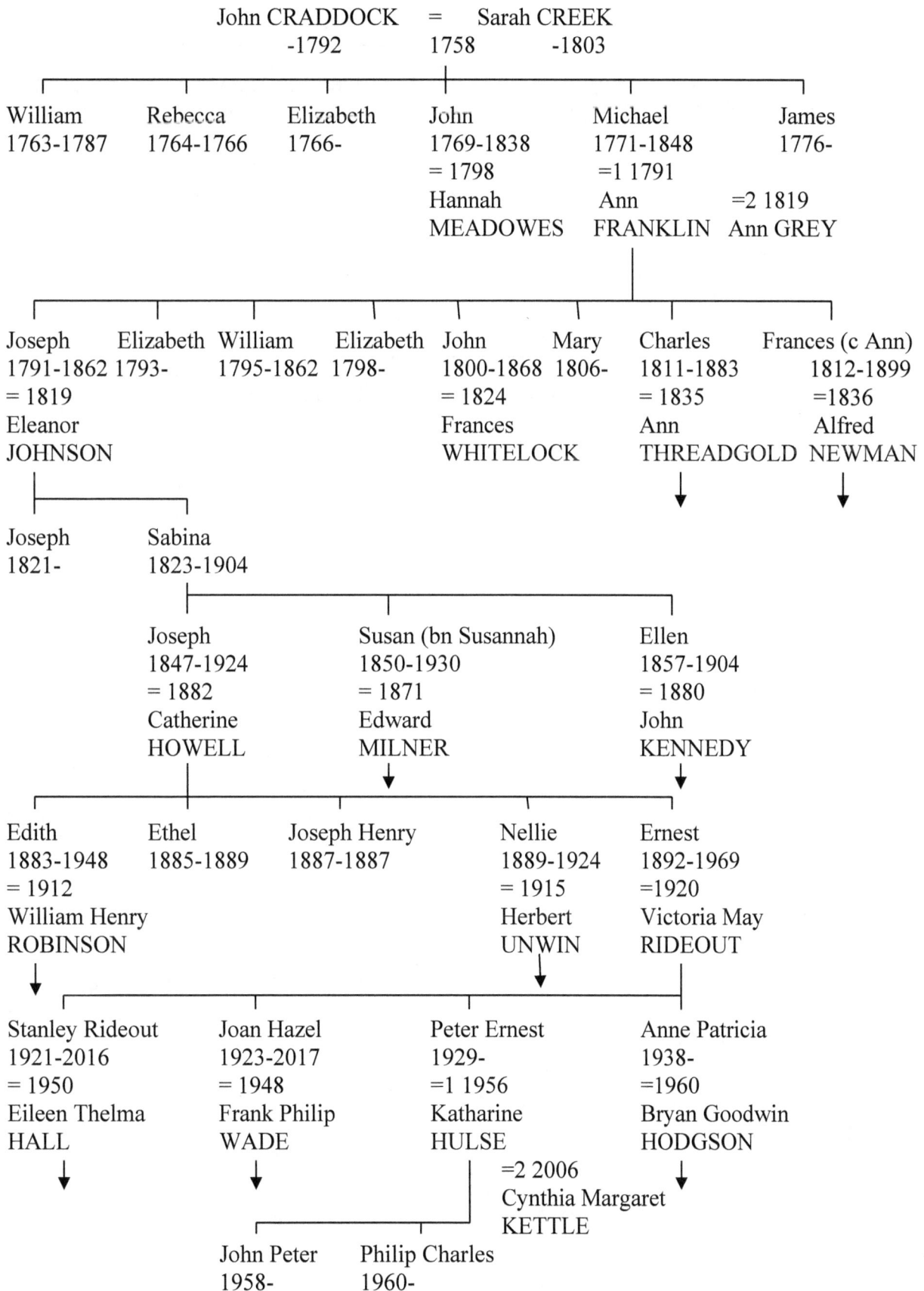

Family Trees

John CRADDOCK   =   Sarah CREEK
-1792   1758   -1803

William	Rebecca	Elizabeth	John	Michael	James
1763-1787	1764-1766	1766-	1769-1838	1771-1848	1776-
			= 1798	=1 1791	
			Hannah	Ann	=2 1819
			MEADOWES	FRANKLIN	Ann GREY

Joseph	Elizabeth	William	Elizabeth	John	Mary	Charles	Frances (c Ann)
1791-1862	1793-	1795-1862	1798-	1800-1868	1806-	1811-1883	1812-1899
= 1819				= 1824		= 1835	=1836
Eleanor				Frances		Ann	Alfred
JOHNSON				WHITELOCK		THREADGOLD	NEWMAN

Joseph	Sabina
1821-	1823-1904

Joseph	Susan (bn Susannah)	Ellen
1847-1924	1850-1930	1857-1904
= 1882	= 1871	= 1880
Catherine	Edward	John
HOWELL	MILNER	KENNEDY

Edith	Ethel	Joseph Henry	Nellie	Ernest
1883-1948	1885-1889	1887-1887	1889-1924	1892-1969
= 1912			= 1915	=1920
William Henry			Herbert	Victoria May
ROBINSON			UNWIN	RIDEOUT

Stanley Rideout	Joan Hazel	Peter Ernest	Anne Patricia
1921-2016	1923-2017	1929-	1938-
= 1950	= 1948	=1 1956	=1960
Eileen Thelma	Frank Philip	Katharine	Bryan Goodwin
HALL	WADE	HULSE	HODGSON
		=2 2006	
		Cynthia Margaret	
		KETTLE	

John Peter	Philip Charles
1958-	1960-

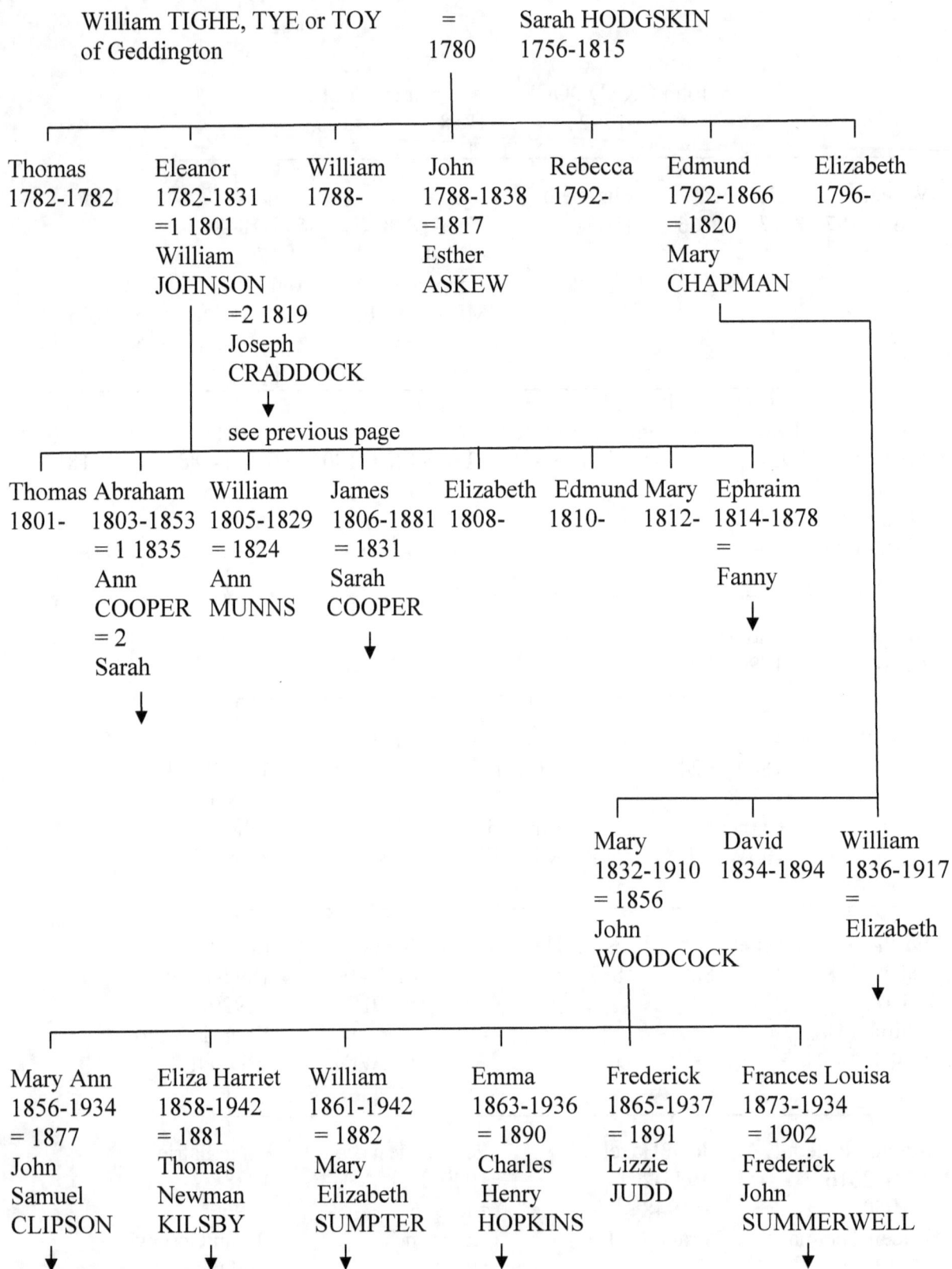

William TIGHE, TYE or TOY   =   Sarah HODGSKIN
of Geddington   1780   1756-1815

Thomas   Eleanor   William   John   Rebecca   Edmund   Elizabeth
1782-1782   1782-1831   1788-   1788-1838   1792-   1792-1866   1796-
            =1 1801   =1817   = 1820
            William   Esther   Mary
            JOHNSON   ASKEW   CHAPMAN
                =2 1819
            Joseph
            CRADDOCK

            ↓
            see previous page

Thomas Abraham   William   James   Elizabeth   Edmund   Mary   Ephraim
1801-   1803-1853   1805-1829   1806-1881   1808-   1810-   1812-   1814-1878
        = 1 1835   = 1824   = 1831   =
        Ann   Ann   Sarah
        COOPER   MUNNS   COOPER   Fanny
        = 2   ↓   ↓
        Sarah

          ↓

                                        Mary   David   William
                                        1832-1910   1834-1894   1836-1917
                                        = 1856   =
                                        John   Elizabeth
                                        WOODCOCK   ↓

Mary Ann   Eliza Harriet   William   Emma   Frederick   Frances Louisa
1856-1934   1858-1942   1861-1942   1863-1936   1865-1937   1873-1934
= 1877   = 1881   = 1882   = 1890   = 1891   = 1902
John   Thomas   Mary   Charles   Lizzie   Frederick
Samuel   Newman   Elizabeth   Henry   JUDD   John
CLIPSON   KILSBY   SUMPTER   HOPKINS   SUMMERWELL
   ↓   ↓   ↓   ↓   ↓

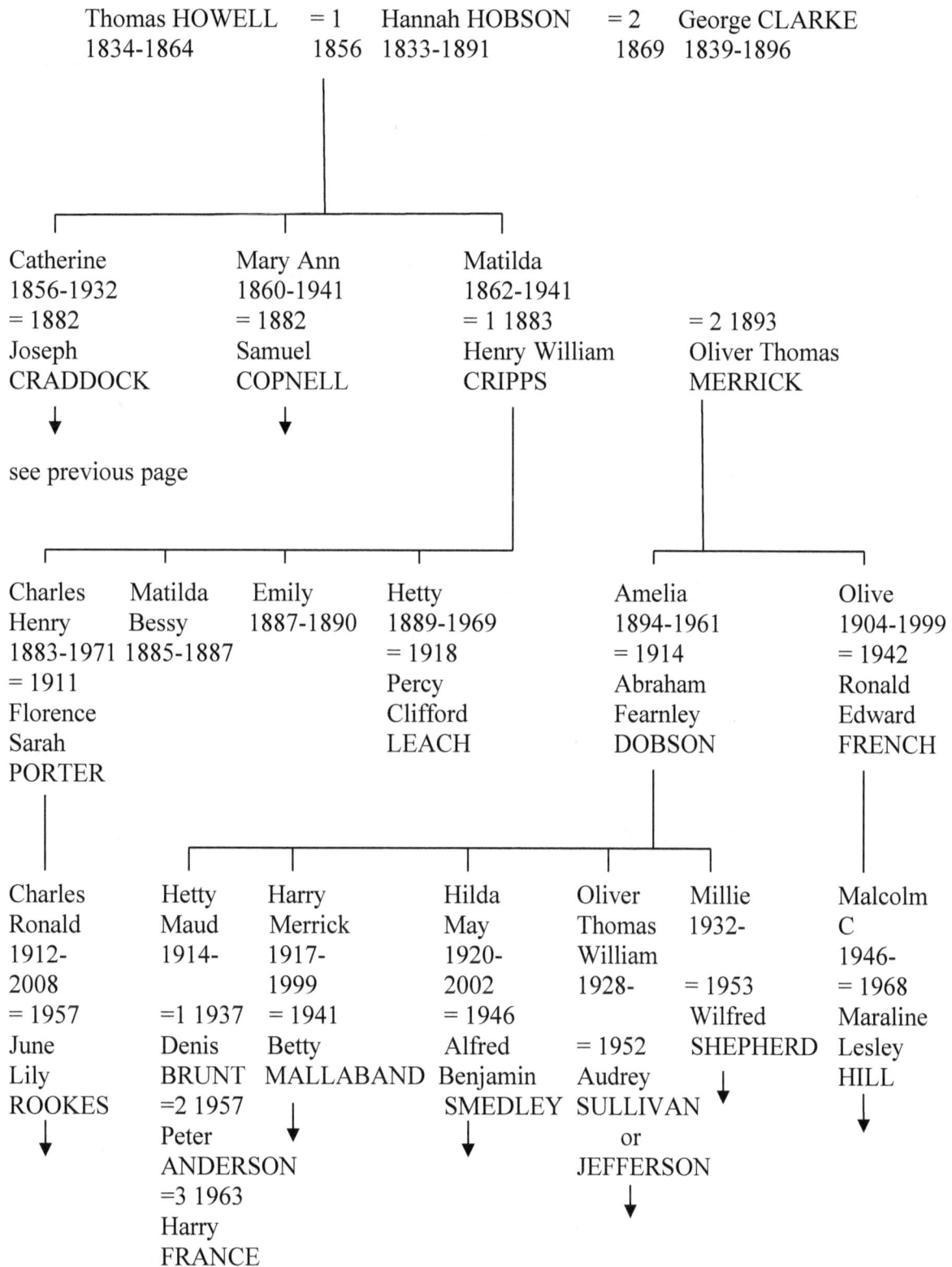

Thomas HOWELL   = 1   Hannah HOBSON   = 2   George CLARKE
1834-1864   1856   1833-1891   1869   1839-1896

Catherine	Mary Ann	Matilda	
1856-1932	1860-1941	1862-1941	
= 1882	= 1882	= 1 1883	= 2 1893
Joseph	Samuel	Henry William	Oliver Thomas
CRADDOCK	COPNELL	CRIPPS	MERRICK
↓	↓		

see previous page

Charles Henry	Matilda Bessy	Emily	Hetty	Amelia	Olive
1883-1971	1885-1887	1887-1890	1889-1969	1894-1961	1904-1999
= 1911			= 1918	= 1914	= 1942
Florence			Percy	Abraham	Ronald
Sarah			Clifford	Fearnley	Edward
PORTER			LEACH	DOBSON	FRENCH

Charles Ronald	Hetty Maud	Harry Merrick	Hilda May	Oliver Thomas William	Millie	Malcolm C
1912-2008	1914-	1917-1999	1920-2002	1928-	1932-	1946-
= 1957	=1 1937	= 1941	= 1946		= 1953	= 1968
June	Denis	Betty	Alfred	= 1952	Wilfred	Maraline
Lily	BRUNT	MALLABAND	Benjamin	Audrey	SHEPHERD	Lesley
ROOKES	=2 1957	↓	SMEDLEY	SULLIVAN	↓	HILL
↓	Peter		↓	or		↓
	ANDERSON			JEFFERSON		
	=3 1963			↓		
	Harry					
	FRANCE					

Bibliography

Barnes, E.G., The Midland Main Line 1875-1922
George Allen & Unwin Ltd., 1969

Craddock, John Peter, He Soldiered under Kitchener,
The Life and Times of Private Harry Milner of Darley Dale
Privately produced, 1992

Craddock, J.P., Sheffield Hero, The Life of Capt. Matt Sheppard
Pickard Communication, 2007

Craddock, J.P., William Henry Robinson, Sheffield Schoolmaster & Educationist
Cade Books, 2018

Craddock, Stanley Rideout, Ernest Craddock 1892-1969, A Short Biography
Privately produced, 1994

Fox, Peter, Steam Days on BR – 1 The Midland Line in Sheffield
Platform 5 Publishing Ltd., 1990

Ireson, Tony, Old Kettering – A view from the 1930s
Published by the author, Book 1 1988, Book 2 1990,
Book 3 1992, Book 4 1994, Book 5 1997, Book 6 1999

Jenkins, Eric, Workhouse Tales, True Stories of the Victorian Poor Law
Cordelia, 1998

McKillop, Norman, The Lighted Flame, A History of the Associated Society
of Locomotive Engineers and Firemen
Thomas Nelson and Sons Ltd, 1950

Partridge, L., A Portrait of Kettering in the Age of Reform, 1800-1850
Kettering Civic Society, 1981

Payne, Jeanne, One Hundred Years of Cranford, Northamptonshire,
People and Organizations: History, Photographs and
Memories of Villagers, Friends and Family, 2010

www.ingramcontent.com/pod-product-compliance
Lightning Source LLC
LaVergne TN
LVHW081450070426
835511LV00013B/1922